FAMILY ISSUES IN THE 21ST CENTURY

COST OF RAISING A CHILD

FAMILY EXPENDITURE REPORTS 2011-2012

FAMILY ISSUES IN THE 21ST CENTURY

Additional books in this series can be found on Nova's website under the Series tab.

Additional E-books in this series can be found on Nova's website under the E-book tab.

ECONOMIC ISSUES, PROBLEMS AND PERSPECTIVES

Additional books in this series can be found on Nova's website under the Series tab.

Additional E-books in this series can be found on Nova's website under the E-book tab.

FAMILY ISSUES IN THE 21ST CENTURY

COST OF RAISING A CHILD

FAMILY EXPENDITURE REPORTS 2011-2012

ATHENA M. BYERS
EDITOR

New York

For permission to use material from this book please contact us:
Telephone 631-231-7269; Fax 631-231-8175
Web Site: http://www.novapublishers.com

LIBRARY OF CONGRESS CATALOGING-IN-PUBLICATION DATA

ISBN: 978-1-62948-369-6

Published by Nova Science Publishers, Inc. † New York

CONTENTS

PREFACE

Chapter 1 – Since 1960, the U.S. Department of Agriculture has provided estimates of expenditures on children from birth through age 17. This technical report presents the most recent estimates for husband-wife and single-parent families using data from the 2005-06 Consumer Expenditure Survey, updated to 2012 dollars using the Consumer Price Index. Data and methods used in calculating annual child-rearing expenses are described. Estimates are provided for major components of the budget by age of child, family income, and region of residence. For the overall United States, annual child-rearing expense estimates ranged between $12,600 and $14,700 for a child in a two-child, married-couple family in the middle-income group. Adjustment factors for number of children in the household are also provided. Results of this study should be of use in developing State child support and foster care guidelines, as well as in family educational programs.

Chapter 2 – Since 1960, the U.S. Department of Agriculture has provided estimates of expenditures on children from birth through age 17. This technical report presents the most recent estimates for husband-wife and single-parent families using data from the 2005-06 Consumer Expenditure Survey, updated to 2011 dollars using the Consumer Price Index. Data and methods used in calculating annual child-rearing expenses are described. Estimates are provided for major components of the budget by age of child, family income, and region of residence. For the overall United States, annual child-rearing expense estimates ranged between $12,290 and $14,320 for a child in a two-child, married-couple family in the middle-income group. Adjustment factors for number of children in the household are also provided. Results of this study should be of use in developing State child support and foster care guidelines, as well as in family educational programs.

In: Cost of Raising a Child
Editor: Athena M. Byers

ISBN: 978-1-62948-369-6

Chapter 1

EXPENDITURES ON CHILDREN BY FAMILIES, 2012*

Mark Lino

ABSTRACT

Since 1960, the U.S. Department of Agriculture has provided estimates of expenditures on children from birth through age 17. This technical report presents the most recent estimates for husband-wife and single-parent families using data from the 2005-06 Consumer Expenditure Survey, updated to 2012 dollars using the Consumer Price Index. Data and methods used in calculating annual child-rearing expenses are described. Estimates are provided for major components of the budget by age of child, family income, and region of residence. For the overall United States, annual child-rearing expense estimates ranged between $12,600 and $14,700 for a child in a two-child, married-couple family in the middle-income group. Adjustment factors for number of children in the household are also provided. Results of this study should be of use in developing State child support and foster care guidelines, as well as in family educational programs.

* This is an edited, reformatted and augmented version of the U.S. Department of Agriculture, Center for Nutrition Policy and Promotion. Miscellaneous Publication No. 1528-2012, dated August, 2013.

EXECUTIVE SUMMARY

Since 1960, the U.S Department of Agriculture (USDA) has provided estimates of annual expenditures on children from birth through age 17. This technical report presents the 2012 estimates for husband-wife and single-parent families. Results are shown in tables 1-7 at the end of this report. Expenditures are provided by age of children, household income level, major budgetary component (housing, food, etc.), and region (for husband-wife families).

Methods

Data used to estimate expenditures on children are from the 2005-06 Consumer Expenditure Survey—Interview portion (CE). Administered by the U.S. Census Bureau, U.S. Department of Commerce, under contract with the Bureau of Labor Statistics (BLS), U.S. Department of Labor, this survey is the most comprehensive source of information on household expenditures available at the national level. The sample consisted of 11,800 husband-wife households and 3,350 single-parent households and was weighted to reflect the U.S. population of interest by using BLS weighting methods.

The CE collects overall household expenditure data for some budgetary components (housing, food, transportation, health care, and miscellaneous goods and services) and child-specific expenditure data for other components (clothing, child care, and education). Child-specific expenses were allocated directly to children. Food and health care expenses were allocated to children based on findings from Federal surveys on children's budget shares. Family-related transportation expenses and miscellaneous expenses were allocated by using a per capita method. This method is preferable over a marginal cost method that measures child-rearing expenditures as the difference in expenses between equivalent couples with and without children. The average cost of an additional bedroom approach was used to estimate housing expenses on a child.

Although based on the 2005-06 CE, the expense estimates were updated to 2012 dollars by using the Consumer Price Index (CPI) for specific budgetary components: 2005 expenditure and income data were first converted to 2006 dollars to complete the analysis and then the results were updated to 2012 dollars.

Table 1. Estimated annual expenditures on a child by husband-wife families, overall United States, 2012

Age of child	Total expense	Housing	Food	Transportation	Clothing	Health care	Child care and education[a]	Miscellaneous[b]
Before tax income: Less than $60,640 (Average = $38,790)								
0 - 2	$9,290	$3,040	$1,190	$1,200	$660	$650	$2,120	$430
3 - 5	9,340	3,040	1,300	1,250	520	610	1,990	630
6 - 8	8,990	3,040	1,760	1,380	590	690	890	640
9 - 11	9,780	3,040	2,020	1,390	600	740	1,350	640
12 - 14	10,200	3,040	2,190	1,510	710	1,130	910	710
15 - 17	10,230	3,040	2,180	1,670	750	1,050	950	590
Total	**$173,490**	**$54,720**	**$31,920**	**$25,200**	**$11,490**	**$14,610**	**$24,630**	**$10,920**
Before-tax income: $60,640 to $105,000 (Average = $81,600)								
0 - 2	$12,710	$3,990	$1,430	$1,730	$790	$880	$2,980	$910
3 - 5	12,720	3,990	1,530	1,780	630	830	2,850	1,110
6 - 8	12,600	3,990	2,150	1,910	710	970	1,750	1,120
9 - 11	13,450	3,990	2,460	1,910	730	1,040	2,200	1,120
12 - 14	14,180	3,990	2,640	2,040	870	1,460	1,990	1,190
15 - 17	14,700	3,990	2,630	2,200	930	1,380	2,500	1,070
Total	**$241,080**	**$71,820**	**$38,520**	**$34,710**	**$13,980**	**$19,680**	**$42,810**	**$19,560**
Before-tax income: More than $105,000 (Average = $183,770)								
0 - 2	$21,000	$7,220	$1,950	$2,610	$1,090	$1,010	$5,300	$1,820
3 - 5	21,000	7,220	2,050	2,670	910	960	5,170	2,020
6 - 8	20,930	7,220	2,700	2,790	1,000	1,120	4,070	2,030
9 - 11	21,870	7,220	3,060	2,800	1,040	1,190	4,530	2,030
12 - 14	23,280	7,220	3,270	2,920	1,210	1,670	4,890	2,100

Table 1. (Continued)

Age of child	Total expense	Housing	Food	Transportation	Clothing	Health care	Child care and education[a]	Miscellaneous[b]
15 - 17	25,180	7,220	3,260	3,090	1,320	1,580	6,730	1,980
Total	**$399,780**	**$129,960**	**$48,870**	**$50,640**	**$19,710**	**$22,590**	**$92,070**	**$35,940**

Estimates are based on 2005-06 Consumer Expenditure Survey data updated to 2012 dollars by using the Consumer Price Index. For each age category, the expense estimates represent average child-rearing expenditures for each age (e.g., the expense for the 3-5 age category, on average, applies to the 3-year-old, the 4-year-old, or the 5-year-old). The Total (0 - 17) row represents the expenditure sum of all ages (0, 1, 2, 3, ...17) in 2012 dollars. The figures represent estimated expenses on the younger child in a two-child family. Estimates are about the same for the older child, so to calculate expenses for two children, figures should be summed for the appropriate age categories. To estimate expenses for an only child, multiply the total expense for the appropriate age category by 1.25. To estimate expenses for each child in a family with three or more children, multiply the total expense for each appropriate age category by 0.78.

For expenses on all children in a family, these totals should be summed.

[a] Includes only families with child care and education expenses.

[b] Includes personal care items, entertainment, and reading materials.

Table 2. Estimated annual expenditures on a child by husband-wife families, urban Northeast, 2012

Age of child	Total expense	Housing	Food	Transportation	Clothing	Health care	Child care and education[a]	Miscellaneous[b]
Before-tax income: Less than $60,850 (Average = $38,920)								
0 - 2	$11,030	$3,620	$1,270	$1,130	$740	$580	$3,250	$440
3 - 5	11,040	3,620	1,370	1,190	580	550	3,080	650
6 - 8	10,700	3,620	1,850	1,320	660	610	1,970	670

Age of child	Total expense	Housing	Food	Transportation	Clothing	Health care	Child care and education[a]	Miscellaneous[b]
9 - 11	11,490	3,620	2,140	1,320	680	660	2,410	660
12 - 14	12,240	3,620	2,310	1,450	820	1,010	2,300	730
15 - 17	13,000	3,620	2,310	1,610	880	940	3,030	610
Total	**$208,500**	**$65,160**	**$33,750**	**$24,060**	**$13,080**	**$13,050**	**$48,120**	**$11,280**
Before-tax income: $60,850 to $105,360 (Average = $81,880)								
0 - 2	$14,520	$4,750	$1,500	$1,670	$880	$790	$4,010	$920
3 - 5	14,480	4,750	1,600	1,730	700	750	3,830	1,120
6 - 8	14,400	4,750	2,250	1,860	790	880	2,730	1,140
9 - 11	15,250	4,750	2,570	1,860	820	940	3,170	1,140
12 - 14	16,270	4,750	2,770	1,990	990	1,320	3,240	1,210
15 - 17	17,470	4,750	2,760	2,150	1,080	1,240	4,400	1,090
Total	**$277,170**	**$85,500**	**$40,350**	**$33,780**	**$15,780**	**$17,760**	**$64,140**	**$19,860**
Before-tax income: More than $105,360 (Average = $184,440)								
0 - 2	$23,400	$8,600	$2,020	$2,560	$1,190	$930	$6,280	$1,820
3 - 5	23,360	8,600	2,120	2,620	1,000	880	6,110	2,030
6 - 8	23,290	8,600	2,780	2,750	1,090	1,020	5,000	2,050
9 - 11	24,230	8,600	3,160	2,750	1,140	1,090	5,440	2,050
12 - 14	25,950	8,600	3,380	2,880	1,350	1,530	6,090	2,120
15 - 17	28,470	8,600	3,370	3,030	1,490	1,440	8,540	2,000
Total	**$446,100**	**$154,800**	**$50,490**	**$49,770**	**$21,780**	**$20,670**	**$112,380**	**$36,210**

Estimates are based on 2005-06 Consumer Expenditure Survey data updated to 2012 dollars by using the regional Consumer Price Index. For each age category, the expense estimates represent average child-rearing expenditures for each age (e.g., the expense for the 3-5 age category, on average, applies to the 3-year-old, the 4-year-old, or the 5-year-old). The Total (0 - 17) row represents the expenditure sum of all ages (0, 1, 2, 3, ...17) in 2012 dollars. The figures represent estimated expenses on the younger child in a two-child family. Estimates are about the same for the older child, so to calculate expenses for two children, figures should be summed for the appropriate age categories. To estimate expenses for an only child, multiply the total expense for the appropriate age category by 1.25. To estimate expenses for each child in a family with three or more children, multiply the total expense for each appropriate age category by 0.78. For expenses on all children in a family, these totals should be summed.

The Northeastern region consists of Connecticut, Maine, Massachusetts, New Hampshire, New Jersey, New York, Pennsylvania, Rhode Island, and Vermont.

[a] Includes only families with child care and education expenses.

[b] Includes personal care items, entertainment, and reading materials.

Table 3. Estimated annual expenditures on a child by husband-wife families, urban West, 2012

Age of child	Total expense	Housing	Food	Transportation	Clothing	Health care	Child care and education[a]	Miscellaneous[b]
Before-tax income: Less than \$60,160 (Average = \$38,480)								
0 - 2	\$10,140	\$3,630	\$1,240	\$1,300	\$700	\$600	\$2,110	\$560
3 - 5	10,140	3,630	1,340	1,350	560	560	1,940	760
6 - 8	9,790	3,630	1,810	1,480	630	630	830	780
9 - 11	10,590	3,630	2,090	1,490	650	680	1,270	780
12 - 14	11,030	3,630	2,260	1,610	770	1,040	870	850
15 - 17	11,120	3,630	2,250	1,770	820	960	960	730
Total	**\$188,430**	**\$65,340**	**\$32,970**	**\$27,000**	**\$12,390**	**\$13,410**	**\$23,940**	**\$13,380**
Before-tax income: \$60,160 to \$104,160 (Average = \$80,940)								
0 - 2	\$13,600	\$4,760	\$1,470	\$1,830	\$830	\$820	\$2,860	\$1,030
3 - 5	13,580	4,760	1,570	1,890	670	770	2,690	1,230
6 - 8	13,470	4,760	2,200	2,020	750	900	1,590	1,250
9 - 11	14,320	4,760	2,510	2,020	780	970	2,030	1,250

Age of child	Total expense	Housing	Food	Transportation	Clothing	Health care	Child care and education[a]	Miscellaneous[b]
12 - 14	15,030	4,760	2,700	2,150	930	1,360	1,810	1,320
15 - 17	15,570	4,760	2,690	2,300	1,010	1,280	2,330	1,200
Total	**$256,710**	**$85,680**	**$39,420**	**$36,630**	**$14,910**	**$18,300**	**$39,930**	**$21,840**
Before-tax income: More than $104,160 (Average = $182,290)								
0 - 2	$22,460	$8,620	$1,970	$2,710	$1,140	$950	$5,140	$1,930
3 - 5	22,420	8,620	2,070	2,770	960	900	4,970	2,130
6 - 8	22,350	8,620	2,720	2,900	1,050	1,050	3,860	2,150
9 - 11	23,270	8,620	3,090	2,900	1,090	1,120	4,300	2,150
12 - 14	24,690	8,620	3,300	3,030	1,290	1,570	4,660	2,220
15 - 17	26,550	8,620	3,290	3,190	1,400	1,480	6,470	2,100
Total	**$425,220**	**$155,160**	**$49,320**	**$52,500**	**$20,790**	**$21,210**	**$88,200**	**$38,040**

Estimates are based on 2005-06 Consumer Expenditure Survey data updated to 2012 dollars by using the regional Consumer Price Index. For each age category, the expense estimates represent average child-rearing expenditures for each age (e.g., the expense for the 3-5 age category, on average, applies to the 3-year-old, the 4-year-old, or the 5-year-old). The Total (0 - 17) row represents the expenditure sum of all ages (0, 1, 2, 3, ...17) in 2012 dollars. The figures represent estimated expenses on the younger child in a two-child family. Estimates are about the same for the older child, so to calculate expenses for two children, figures should be summed for the appropriate age categories. To estimate expenses for an only child, multiply the total expense for the appropriate age category by 1.25. To estimate expenses for each child in a family with three or more children, multiply the total expense for each appropriate age category by 0.78. For expenses on all children in a family, these totals should be summed.

The Western region consists of Alaska, Arizona, California, Colorado, Hawaii, Idaho, Montana, Nevada, New Mexico, Oregon, Utah, Washington, and Wyoming.

[a] Includes only families with child care and education expenses.

[b] Includes personal care items, entertainment, and reading materials.

Table 4. Estimated annual expenditures on a child by husband-wife families, urban Midwest, 2012

Age of child	Total expense	Housing	Food	Transportation	Clothing	Health care	Child care and education[a]	Miscellaneous[b]
Before-tax income: Less than $60,450 (Average = $38,670)								
0 - 2	$9,180	$2,920	$1,130	$1,120	$650	$620	$2,260	$480
3 - 5	9,180	2,920	1,230	1,180	500	580	2,080	690
6 - 8	8,830	2,920	1,680	1,310	580	650	980	710
9 - 11	9,600	2,920	1,950	1,320	590	700	1,420	700
12 - 14	10,100	2,920	2,120	1,440	710	1,070	1,060	780
15 - 17	10,250	2,920	2,110	1,600	750	990	1,220	660
Total	**$171,420**	**$52,560**	**$30,660**	**$23,910**	**$11,340**	**$13,830**	**$27,060**	**$12,060**
Before-tax income: $60,450 to $104,670 (Average = $81,340)								
0 - 2	$12,450	$3,830	$1,370	$1,660	$780	$840	$3,010	$960
3 - 5	12,430	3,830	1,470	1,720	620	790	2,830	1,170
6 - 8	12,310	3,830	2,080	1,850	700	930	1,730	1,190
9 - 11	13,140	3,830	2,390	1,860	720	990	2,170	1,180
12 - 14	13,900	3,830	2,570	1,980	870	1,400	2,000	1,250
15 - 17	14,500	3,830	2,560	2,140	940	1,310	2,590	1,130
Total	**$236,190**	**$68,940**	**$37,320**	**$33,630**	**$13,890**	**$18,780**	**$42,990**	**$20,640**
Before-tax income: More than $104,670 (Average = $183,180)								
0 - 2	$20,600	$6,940	$1,880	$2,560	$1,080	$980	$5,290	$1,870
3 - 5	20,540	6,940	1,980	2,620	890	930	5,110	2,070
6 - 8	20,480	6,940	2,620	2,750	980	1,080	4,010	2,100
9 - 11	21,380	6,940	2,980	2,750	1,020	1,150	4,450	2,090
12 - 14	22,840	6,940	3,190	2,880	1,210	1,610	4,850	2,160

Age of child	Total expense	Housing	Food	Transportation	Clothing	Health care	Child care and education[a]	Miscellaneous[b]
15 - 17	24,760	6,940	3,180	3,030	1,320	1,520	6,730	2,040
Total	**$391,800**	**$124,920**	**$47,490**	**$49,770**	**$19,500**	**$21,810**	**$91,320**	**$36,990**

Estimates are based on 2005-06 Consumer Expenditure Survey data updated to 2012 dollars by using the regional Consumer Price Index. For each age category, the expense estimates represent average child-rearing expenditures for each age (e.g., the expense for the 3-5 age category, on average, applies to the 3-year-old, the 4-year-old, or the 5-year-old). The Total (0 - 17) row represents the expenditure sum of all ages (0, 1, 2, 3, ...17) in 2012 dollars. The figures represent estimated expenses on the younger child in a two-child family. Estimates are about the same for the older child, so to calculate expenses for two children, figures should be summed for the appropriate age categories. To estimate expenses for an only child, multiply the total expense for the appropriate age category by 1.25. To estimate expenses for each child in a family with three or more children, multiply the total expense for each appropriate age category by 0.78. For expenses on all children in a family, these totals should be summed.

The Midwestern region consists of Illinois, Indiana, Iowa, Kansas, Michigan, Minnesota, Missouri, Nebraska, North Dakota, Ohio, South Dakota, and Wisconsin.

[a] Includes only families with child care and education expenses.

[b] Includes personal care items, entertainment, and reading materials.

Table 5. Estimated annual expenditures on a child by husband-wife families, urban South, 2012

Age of child	Total expense	Housing	Food	Transportation	Clothing	Health care	Child care and education[a]	Miscellaneous[b]
Before-tax income: Less than $61,060 (Average = $39,050)								
0 - 2	$8,710	$2,750	$1,190	$1,150	$640	$610	$2,060	$310
3 - 5	8,730	2,750	1,300	1,210	500	570	1,890	510
6 - 8	8,370	2,750	1,760	1,340	570	640	780	530
9 - 11	9,150	2,750	2,040	1,340	580	690	1,220	530

Table 5. (Continued)

Age of child	Total expense	Housing	Food	Transportation	Clothing	Health care	Child care and education[a]	Miscellaneous[b]
12 - 14	9,590	2,750	2,210	1,470	700	1,050	810	600
15 - 17	9,650	2,750	2,200	1,630	740	980	870	480
Total	**$162,600**	**$49,500**	**$32,100**	**$24,420**	**$11,190**	**$13,620**	**$22,890**	**$8,880**
Before-tax income: $61,060 to $105,720 (Average = $82,150)								
0 - 2	$11,920	$3,610	$1,430	$1,690	$760	$830	$2,820	$780
3 - 5	11,900	3,610	1,530	1,750	610	780	2,640	980
6 - 8	11,780	3,610	2,160	1,880	680	910	1,540	1,000
9 - 11	12,640	3,610	2,470	1,890	710	980	1,980	1,000
12 - 14	13,340	3,610	2,660	2,020	850	1,380	1,750	1,070
15 - 17	13,840	3,610	2,660	2,170	920	1,290	2,240	950
Total	**$226,260**	**$64,980**	**$38,730**	**$34,200**	**$13,590**	**$18,510**	**$38,910**	**$17,340**
Before-tax income: More than $105,720 (Average = $185,010)								
0 - 2	$19,850	$6,530	$1,950	$2,590	$1,050	$960	$5,090	$1,680
3 - 5	19,810	6,530	2,050	2,650	870	910	4,920	1,880
6 - 8	19,740	6,530	2,700	2,780	960	1,060	3,810	1,900
9 - 11	20,660	6,530	3,060	2,790	1,000	1,130	4,250	1,900
12 - 14	22,060	6,530	3,280	2,910	1,180	1,590	4,600	1,970
15 - 17	23,890	6,530	3,270	3,070	1,290	1,500	6,380	1,850
Total	**$378,030**	**$117,540**	**$48,930**	**$50,370**	**$19,050**	**$21,450**	**$87,150**	**$33,540**

Estimates are based on 2005-06 Consumer Expenditure Survey data updated to 2012 dollars by using the regional Consumer Price Index. For each age category, the expense estimates represent average child-rearing expenditures for each age (e.g., the expense for the 3-5 age category, on average, applies to the 3-year-old, the 4-year-old, or the 5-year-old). The Total (0 - 17) row represents the expenditure sum of all ages (0, 1, 2, 3, ...17) in 2012 dollars. The figures represent estimated expenses on the younger child in a two-child family. Estimates are about the same for the older child, so to calculate expenses for two children, figures should be summed for the appropriate age categories. To estimate expenses for an only child, multiply the total expense for the appropriate age category by 1.25. To estimate expenses for each child in a family with three or more children, multiply the total expense for each appropriate age category by 0.78. For expenses on all children in a family, these totals should be summed.

The Southern region consists of Alabama, Arkansas, Delaware, District of Columbia, Florida, Georgia, Kentucky, Louisiana, Maryland, Mississippi, North Carolina, Oklahoma, South Carolina, Tennessee, Texas, Virginia, and West Virginia.

[a] Includes only families with child care and education expenses.

[b] Includes personal care items, entertainment, and reading materials.

Table 6. Estimated annual expenditures on a child by husband-wife families, rural areas, 2012

Age of child	Total expense	Housing	Food	Transportation	Clothing	Health care	Child care and education[a]	Miscellaneous[b]
Before-tax income: Less than $61,590 (Average = $39,390)								
0 - 2	$7,830	$1,880	$1,050	$1,310	$650	$640	$1,910	$390
3 - 5	7,400	1,880	1,150	1,370	510	610	1,280	600
6 - 8	7,550	1,880	1,590	1,500	580	680	700	620
9 - 11	7,830	1,880	1,850	1,500	590	730	670	610
12 - 14	8,460	1,880	2,010	1,630	700	1,110	440	690
15 - 17	8,650	1,880	2,010	1,790	740	1,030	640	560
Total	**$143,160**	**$33,840**	**$28,980**	**$27,300**	**$11,310**	**$14,400**	**$16,920**	**$10,410**
Before-tax income: $61,590 to $106,640 (Average = $82,870)								
0 - 2	$10,230	$2,460	$1,300	$1,860	$770	$870	$2,100	$870
3 – 5	9,750	2,460	1,400	1,910	620	820	1,460	1,080

Table 6. (Continued)

Age of child	Total expense	Housing	Food	Transportation	Clothing	Health care	Child care and education[a]	Miscellaneous[b]
6 - 8	10,150	2,460	1,990	2,050	700	960	890	1,100
9 - 11	10,500	2,460	2,290	2,050	720	1,030	860	1,090
12 - 14	11,240	2,460	2,470	2,180	850	1,440	680	1,160
15 - 17	11,560	2,460	2,460	2,340	920	1,360	980	1,040
Total	**$190,290**	**$44,280**	**$35,730**	**$37,170**	**$13,740**	**$19,440**	**$20,910**	**$19,020**
Before-tax income: More than $106,640 (Average = $186,630)								
0 - 2	$16,170	$4,460	$1,820	$2,760	$1,070	$1,010	$3,270	$1,780
3 - 5	15,680	4,460	1,920	2,820	900	960	2,630	1,990
6 - 8	16,100	4,460	2,540	2,950	980	1,110	2,050	2,010
9 - 11	16,520	4,460	2,890	2,950	1,020	1,180	2,020	2,000
12 - 14	17,710	4,460	3,100	3,080	1,200	1,660	2,130	2,080
15 - 17	18,700	4,460	3,090	3,240	1,300	1,560	3,100	1,950
Total	**$302,640**	**$80,280**	**$46,080**	**$53,400**	**$19,410**	**$22,440**	**$45,600**	**$35,430**

Estimates are based on 2005-06 Consumer Expenditure Survey data updated to 2012 dollars by using the population size Consumer Price Index. For each age category, the expense estimates represent average child-rearing expenditures for each age (e.g., the expense for the 3-5 age category, on average, applies to the 3-year-old, the 4-year-old, or the 5-year-old). The Total (0 - 17) row represents the expenditure sum of all ages (0, 1, 2, 3, ...17) in 2012 dollars. The figures represent estimated expenses on the younger child in a two-child family. Estimates are about the same for the older child, so to calculate expenses for two children, figures should be summed for the appropriate age categories. To estimate expenses for an only child, multiply the total expense for the appropriate age category by 1.25. To estimate expenses for each child in a family with three or more children, multiply the total expense for each appropriate age category by 0.78. For expenses on all children in a family, these totals should be summed.

Rural areas are places of fewer than 2,500 people outside a Metropolitan Statistical Area.

[a] Includes only families with child care and education expenses.
[b] Includes personal care items, entertainment, and reading materials.

Table 7. Estimated annual expenditures on a child by single-parent families, overall United States, 2012

Age of child	Total expense	Housing	Food	Transportation	Clothing	Health care	Child care and education[a]	Miscellaneous[b]
Before-tax income: Less than $60,640 (Average = $26,900)								
0 - 2	$7,950	$2,880	$1,430	$700	$420	$540	$1,460	$520
3 - 5	8,830	2,880	1,410	940	340	620	2,020	620
6 - 8	8,660	2,880	1,880	1,050	360	690	1,000	800
9 - 11	9,250	2,880	2,060	1,090	420	640	1,410	750
12 - 14	9,660	2,880	2,210	1,160	430	970	1,160	850
15 - 17	9,390	2,880	2,330	1,160	470	960	910	680
Total	**$161,220**	**$51,840**	**$33,960**	**$18,300**	**$7,320**	**$13,260**	**$23,880**	**$12,660**
Before-tax income: $60,640 or more (Average = $110,050)								
0 - 2	$17,190	$5,980	$2,130	$1,960	$610	$1,010	$3,820	$1,680
3 - 5	18,130	5,980	2,130	2,210	520	1,130	4,380	1,780
6 - 8	18,270	5,980	2,750	2,320	540	1,230	3,490	1,960
9 - 11	19,140	5,980	3,080	2,350	630	1,150	4,040	1,910
12 - 14	20,190	5,980	3,160	2,420	680	1,620	4,320	2,010
15 - 17	21,130	5,980	3,310	2,420	750	1,610	5,220	1,840
Total	**$342,150**	**$107,640**	**$49,680**	**$41,040**	**$11,190**	**$23,250**	**$75,810**	**$33,540**

Estimates are based on 2005-06 Consumer Expenditure Survey data updated to 2012 dollars by using the Consumer Price Index. For each age category, the expense estimates represent average child-rearing expenditures for each age (e.g., the expense for the 3-5 age category, on average, applies to the 3-year-old, the 4-year-old, or the 5-year-old). The Total (0 - 17) row represents the expenditure sum of all ages (0, 1, 2, 3, ...17) in 2012 dollars. The figures represent estimated expenses on the younger child in a single-parent, two-child family. For estimated expenses on the older child, multiply the total expense for the appropriate age category by 0.97. To estimate expenses for two children, the expenses on the younger child and older child after adjusting the expense on the older child downward should be summed for the appropriate age categories. To estimate expenses for an only child, multiply the total expense for the appropriate age category by 1.29. To estimate expenses for each child in a family with three or more children, multiply the total expense for each appropriate age category by 0.77 after adjusting the expenses on the older children downward. For expenses on all children in a family, these totals should be summed.

[a] Includes only families with child care and education expenses.

[b] Includes personal care items, entertainment, and reading materials.

Selected Results

- Child-rearing expenses vary considerably by household income level. For a child in a two-child, husband-wife family, annual expenses ranged from $8,990 to $10,230, on average, (depending on age of the child) for households with before-tax income less than $60,640, from $12,600 to $14,700 for households with before-tax income between $60,640 and $105,000, and from $20,930 to $25,180 for households with before-tax income more than $105,000.
- As a proportion of total child-rearing expenses, housing accounted for the largest share across income groups, comprising 30 to 33 percent of total expenses on a child in a two-child, husband-wife family. For families in the middle-income group, child care/education (for those with the expense) and food were the next largest average expenditures on a child, accounting for 18 and 16 percent of child-rearing expenses, respectively.
- Annual expenditures on children generally increased with age of the child. This fact was the same for both husband-wife and single-parent families.
- Overall annual child-rearing expenses were highest for husband-wife families in the urban Northeast, followed by families in the urban West and urban Midwest; families in the urban South and rural areas had the lowest child-rearing expenses.
- Compared with expenditures on each child in a two-child, husband-wife family, expenditures by husband-wife households with one child average 25 percent more on the single child and expenditures by households with three or more children average 22 percent less on each child.
- Child-rearing expense patterns of single-parent households with a before-tax income less than $60,640 were 7 percent lower than those of husband-wife households in the same income group. Most single-parent households were in this income group (compared with about one-third of husband-wife families).

Other Expenditures on Children

Expenditures for major budgetary components estimated in this study consisted of direct parental expenses made on children through age 17. These expenditures exclude college costs and other parental expenses on children after age 17. In addition, expenditures on children made by people outside the household and by the government are not included. Indirect costs involved in child rearing by parents (time costs and foregone earnings and career opportunities) are also not included in the estimates.

EXPENDITURES ON CHILDREN BY FAMILIES, 2012

The U.S. Department of Agriculture (USDA) has provided estimates of expenditures on children from birth through age 17 since 1960. These estimates may be used in developing State child support guidelines and foster care payments, as well as in family education programs. This report presents 2012 estimated child-rearing expenses by husband-wife and single-parent families. The figures for 2012 are shown in tables 1-7 at the end of this report. The 2012 USDA estimates are not directly comparable to previous estimates (U.S. Department of Agriculture, 1981; Lino, 2008) because of changes in methods.

For husband-wife families, child-rearing expenses are for three income groups and for single- parent families, two income groups. To adjust partially for price differentials and varying patterns of expenditures, USDA also provides estimates for husband-wife families in various regions, as well as the United States overall. For single-parent families, estimates are provided only for the United States overall because of limitations in sample size. For all families, expenditures on children are estimated for the major budgetary components: Housing, food, transportation, clothing, health care, child care and education, and miscellaneous goods and services (entertainment, personal care items, etc.).

This report presents the USDA methodology for deriving expenditures on children and the results. First, data used in determining child-rearing expenditures will be described. These data contain overall household expenditures for some budgetary components and child-specific expenditures for other components. Overall household expenditures must be allocated among family members to determine expenses on children. Second, the allocation methods used by USDA will be explained, along with general estimation techniques. Third, an overview of the results will be given. Fourth, how the USDA estimates on child-rearing expenses compare with the results of alternative methodologies on estimating child-rearing expenses will be discussed. The report ends with an explanation of how future child-rearing expenses may be determined and a discussion on other expenses on children not included in this report.

Estimating and Allocating Expenditures on Children

Data Used

Since 1960, the first year USDA produced child-rearing expense estimates, the Consumer Expenditure Survey (CE) has been used as the basis for the estimates. The CE is also used in alternative methodologies on estimating child-rearing expenses. CE data are the most comprehensive source of information on household expenditures available at the national level, containing expenditure data for housing, food, transportation, clothing, health care, child care and education, and miscellaneous goods and services (the box below describes the specific items in each expenditure component).

USDA's latest estimates are based on data from the 2005-06 CE—Interview Survey component. Administered by the U.S. Census Bureau, U.S. Department of Commerce, under contract with the Bureau of Labor Statistics (BLS), U.S. Department of Labor, the CE collects information on characteristics, income, and expenditures of consumer units. For this study, the terms households and families are used for consumer units. During most of 2005-06, about 7,000 to 7,800 households were interviewed each quarter, bringing the total number of interviews in each year's survey to over 28,000. Due to the rotating sample design of the Interview Survey, each sample household could be interviewed up to four consecutive quarters over the 2-year period. Households report expenditures for the 3 months prior to the interview month. Since the households interviewed each quarter are deemed an independent sample by BLS, the 3-month expenditures they report may be annualized (U.S. Department of Labor, 2007) for analytical purposes.

Child-rearing expenses of 11,800 husband-wife and 3,350 single-parent families where the parents were ages 20 to 60 were examined. These households had at least one child of their own, age 17 or under, in the household, and there were no other related or unrelated people present in the household. Most single-parent families (85 percent) were headed by a woman. BLS methods were used to weight all data to reflect the U.S. population of interest.

Although based on 2005-06 data, the expense estimates were updated to 2012 dollars by using the Consumer Price Index (CPI). Expenditure and income data for 2005 were first converted to 2006 dollars, analysis was undertaken, and then the resulting estimations were updated to 2012 dollars. Income levels of households were updated to 2012 dollars by using the all-items category of the CPI, and expenditures were updated by using the CPI for the corresponding budgetary component (i.e., the CPIs for housing, food, etc.). Regional CPIs were used to update the regional estimates, including household income, to 2012 dollars.

CATEGORIES OF HOUSEHOLD EXPENDITURES

Housing expenses consist of shelter (mortgage payments, property taxes, or rent; maintenance and repairs; and insurance), utilities (gas, electricity, fuel, cell/telephone, and water), and house furnishings and equipment (furniture, floor coverings, major appliances, and small appliances). Mortgage payments included principal and interest payments. Overall, principal payments constituted 15 percent of overall housing expenses.

Food expenses consist of food and nonalcoholic beverages purchased at grocery, convenience, and specialty stores, including purchases with Food Stamp Program (now the Supplemental Nutrition Assistance Program) benefits; dining at restaurants; and household expenditures on school meals.

Transportation expenses consist of the monthly payments on vehicle loans, downpayments, gasoline and motor oil, maintenance and repairs, insurance, and public transportation (including airline fares).

Clothing expenses consist of children's apparel such as diapers, shirts, pants, dresses, and suits; footwear; and clothing services such as dry cleaning, alterations, and repair.

Health care expenses consist of medical and dental services not covered by insurance, prescription drugs and medical supplies not covered by insurance, and health insurance premiums not paid by an employer or other organization. Medical services include those related to physical and mental health.

Child care and education expenses consist of day care tuition and supplies; baby-sitting; and elementary and high school tuition, books, fees, and supplies. Books, fees, and supplies may be for private or public schools.

Miscellaneous expenses consist of personal care items (haircuts, toothbrushes, etc.), entertainment (portable media players, sports equipment, televisions, computers, etc.), and reading materials (nonschool books, magazines, etc.).

Although the CE provides the best available data for estimating spending on children, it has its limitations. The CE contains overall household expenditure data for some budgetary components (housing, food, transportation, health care, and miscellaneous goods and services) and child-specific expenditure data for other components (children's clothing, child care, and education). Thus, to estimate child-rearing expenses, these household-level expenditures must be allocated among family members. The next sections describe the methodology used by USDA to allocate these household expenditures. Two different models were used, one to determine food, transportation, health care, clothing, child care and education, and miscellaneous expenses on children, and the other to determine housing expenses on children.

Determining Food, Transportation, Health Care, Clothing, Child Care and Education, and Miscellaneous Expenses on Children

For these budgetary components, multivariate analyses were used to estimate household and child-specific expenditures. These analyses controlled for income level, family size, and age of the younger child so that estimates could be made for families with these varying characteristics. The estimation model, conducted separately for husband-wife and single- parent households, for the overall United States was:

$$E_i = f(Y, HS, CA) \quad (1)$$

where:

E_i = household expenditures on a particular budgetary component (food, transportation, health care, children's clothing, child care and education, and miscellaneous goods and services)

Y = household before-tax income (divided into three groups for husband-wife families: < \$60,640, \$60,640 to \$105,000, and > \$105,000 in 2012 dollars, and two groups for single-parent families: <\$60,640 and \$60,640 or more in 2012 dollars)

HS = number of children in the household (divided into three groups: 1 child, 2 children, and 3 or more children)

CA = age of the younger child (divided into six age groups: 0-2, 3-5, 6-8, 9-11, 12-14, and 15-17)

For the regional estimates of expenditures on children in husband-wife households, the model was:

$$E_i = f(Y, HS, CA, RG) \quad (2)$$

where E_i through CA are the same as before and

RG = region (divided into five regions: urban Northeast, urban South, urban Midwest, urban West, and rural areas)

Ordinary Least Squares analysis was used to estimate expenditures on food, transportation, child care and education, and miscellaneous goods and services. Tobit analysis was used to estimate expenditures on health care and children's clothing because although most households had an expenditure on these budgetary components, over 10 percent reported zero expenses. Because of these zero expenditures, tobit analysis yields statistically better (unbiased) estimates than does Ordinary Least Squares analysis. The procedure outlined by McDonald and Moffitt (1980) was used to transform the estimates resulting from the tobit analysis into dollars. The coefficients of the estimates were used to calculate the expenditures for the budgetary components for each income group, age of the younger child, and region (for husband-wife families) for a two-child family. Households with two children were selected as the standard because two children was the average for husband-wife and single-parent families in 2005-06 based on CE data. Age of the older child was not controlled for because the focus was on the younger child and by doing so, results would only be applicable to families with an older child in a certain age category. It was therefore assumed the distribution of age ranges of the older child was similar across families. Also, additional analysis focused on the older child (see "Adjustments for Older Children and Household Size" section). Typically, the older child was 3 to 4 years older then the younger child and under age 18.

The three income groups of husband-wife households (before-tax income under $60,640, between $60,640 and $105,000, and over $105,000 in 2012 dollars) were determined by dividing the sample of husband-wife families for the overall United States into equal thirds. Income intervals were used to be consistent with previous USDA studies. These three income groups will be referred to as the lower (although most families in this group are above the poverty threshold), middle, and higher income groups. These income groups were also used for the regional analysis of child-rearing expenditures. The regional income groups differ over time because they are being updated with the regional CPIs. Income groups of single-parent households (before-tax income under $60,640 and $60,640 and over in 2012 dollars) were selected to correspond with the income groups used for husband-wife households for comparison purposes, that is, to see how child-rearing expenditures differed between husband-wife and single-parent households in the same income group. This income includes child-support payments. The two higher income groups used with husband-wife families were combined in the case of single-parent families because only 15 percent of these households had a before-tax income of $60,640 and over.

Estimates were made for six age categories of younger children (0-2, 3-5, 6-8, 9-11, 12-14, and 15-17 years) because spending on children differs by age of the child. These age categories approximate the different stages of childhood and have historically been used. The focus was on the younger child in a household because the older child was sometimes over age 17. If the older child had been selected as the household member of interest, expenditures may be different. Also, if households with one or three or more children had been selected, per-child expenditures would reflect the differences in family size. As the number of children in a family increases, the allocation of resources among children changes. To adjust expenditures for the older child and number of children, see discussion beginning on page 15.

For husband-wife families, estimates are provided for the urban Northeast, urban South, urban Midwest, urban West, and rural areas overall, as well as for the overall United States. Urban areas are defined as Metropolitan Statistical Areas (MSAs) and other places of 2,500 or more people outside an MSA; rural areas are places of fewer than 2,500 people outside an MSA. Sample sizes were not sufficient to conduct regional analysis for single-parent families.

Once the expenditures on the budgetary components were estimated, they were allocated to children. The allocation methods varied by budgetary component and are described below.

Clothing

The CE collects data on how much families are spending on children's shoes, pants, dresses, and so on. Hence, estimated expenditures for clothing may be readily assigned to children. It was assumed these expenses were equally allocated to each child in the two-child household when both children were less than age 18. CE data on children's clothing expenditures were for children age 15 and under. For the estimates, it was assumed the clothing expenditures of a 16- or 17-year-old were similar to those of a 15-year-old; thus, these older teenagers were assigned the expenditures of a 15-year-old. Also, expenditures for clothing services (dry cleaning, alterations, etc.), which account for a smaller proportion of total clothing expenses, were esti- mated for the overall household and allocated on a per capita basis among household members.

Child Care and Education

Child care and education was the only budgetary component for which about half of all households reported no expenditure. Expenditure on this budgetary component rose with household income level: For husband-wife families, 31 percent in the lower income group had this expenditure, compared with 45 and 56 percent in the middle and higher income groups; for single-parent families, the percentages were 34 and 44 percent for the lower and higher income groups. Previous USDA estimates of child care/education expenses on a child consisted of households with the expense as well as households without the expense. However, to be more applicable to families, this update included only those families with the expense. For families without child care/education expenses, this budgetary component would amount to zero; therefore, total expenditures on a child should be adjusted to account for this.

As with clothing, estimated expenditures for child care/education in the CE were only for the children in the household so may be readily assigned to them. It was assumed these expenses were equally allocated to each child in the two-child household when both children were less than age 18. For preschool children, most of this budgetary-component expenditure is for child care, whereas for older children, most of this expenditure is for education (a major reason the two components are combined; otherwise, many age categories would have a negligible expense either for one or the other). The child care figures include families with part-time child care on a regular or irregular basis; therefore, they appear low when compared with those with full-time care. For more detailed analysis of average weekly child care expenses for families with the expense, see U.S. Census Bureau (2011). It should be noted that by only including households with child care/education expenses, the total expenses on a child as a result of summing the budgetary components may be overestimated because those with child care/education expenses may have to draw from other child-rearing budgetary components (e.g., housing, transportation, miscellaneous) to pay for it.

Food

Although the CE did not collect expenditures on food by family member, data from the 2008 USDA food plans (U.S. Department of Agriculture, 2008) are used to calculate the shares of total household food expenses spent on children. These shares were used to apportion house- hold food expenses by age of the household member, household size, and income. The USDA food plans are based on household food use and individual intake, as well as food expenditure data. The food plans also reflect the cost of a nutritious diet, which accounts for food costs, nutritional needs, and consumption behavior. These food budget shares, as derived from the USDA food plans, were applied to estimated household food expenditures to determine food expenses on children. The food budget shares ranged between 17 to 25 percent for a child in a two-child, husband-wife family and 25 to 34 percent for a child in a two-child, single-parent family (these shares being higher for a three-person household). Food budget shares generally increased with the age of the child and did not vary much by household income level.

Health Care

Like food, expenditures on health care by family members were not collected by the CE. Data from other sources—in this case, the U.S. Department of Health and Human Services' 2005 Medical Expenditure Panel Survey—show the share of household out-of-pocket health care expenses spent on children. These shares were used to apportion family health care expenses by age of the household member, household size, and income. The Medical Expenditure Panel Survey is a nationally representative longitudinal survey that collects detailed information on health care utilization and expenditures, health insurance, and health status, as well as a wide variety of social, demographic, and economic characteristics for the civilian noninstitutionalized population. (See Bernard, 2007, for more information about this survey, as well as for out-of-pocket expenditures on health care.)

These health care budget shares, as derived from the survey, were applied to estimated house- hold health care expenditures to determine health care expenses on children. The health care budget shares ranged between 16 to 25 percent for a child in a two-child, husband-wife family and 24 to 33 percent for a child in a two-child, single-parent family (these shares again being higher for a three-person household). Health care budget shares generally increased with the age of the child and did not vary much by household income level. As an example of how health care expenditures were calculated on a 6- to 8-year-old, who is the younger child in a husband-wife, two-child household in the middle-income group, overall household health care expenditures were estimated from the multivariate analysis to be $5,390 in 2012 dollars for this family type. Based on the Medical Expenditure Panel Survey, the health care budget share for this 6- to 8-year-old was figured to be 18 percent. Thus, health care expenditures on the 6- to 8-year-old were estimated to be $970 (=$5,390 X 0.18).

Transportation

Transportation expenses related only to family-related activities were examined when determining child-rearing transportation expenses. These activities accounted for 59 percent of total transportation, according to a U.S. Department of Transportation study (Hu & Reuscher, 2004). Other transportation expenses, mainly those due to employment, as well as some household maintenance, are not related directly to expenses on children, so these types of transportation expenses were excluded.

Unlike data for food and health care, no other data show the share of transportation expenses associated with child rearing. Hence, to allocate these expenses, the per capita method was used to determine family-related transportation expenses on a child by allocating in equal proportions the expenses among household members. One of the first studies on child-rearing expenses also used the per capita approach to allocate transportation expenses among family members (Dublin & Lotka, 1946). The per capita method for allocating transportation does not account for some families driving larger vehicles because of children, likely leading to underestimates of transportation expenses on children. Although the per capita method has its limitations, these were judged less severe than those of alternative approaches (see the "Alternative Estimates of Expenditures on Children" section of this report). For a child in a two-child, husband-wife family, the per capita method (factoring in only family-related travel) resulted in approximately 15 percent of total transportation expenses being allocated to the child; for a child in a two-child, single-parent family, 20 percent.

Miscellaneous Expenses

As with expenditures on transportation, no other data show the share of miscellaneous expenses (personal care items, such as haircuts, toothbrushes, etc.; entertainment, such as portable media players, sports equipment, computers, etc.; and reading materials, such as nonschool books, magazines, etc.) attributed to child rearing. Therefore, the per capita method was used to apportion miscellaneous expenses among family members. For many of the goods and services in this budgetary component, such as fees and admissions, videos, and personal care items, the per capita method is reasonable because such goods and services are likely to be equally shared by family members.

Determining Housing Expenses on Children

One method to estimate housing expenses on a child is to track families over time and see how their housing expenses change exclusively as a result of children being added to the household. One would expect families to increase their housing expenditures as they move to larger residences to accommodate children. Child-related housing costs could therefore be calculated by utilizing these additional costs. However, CE data have annual family housing expenses. So, to determine child-rearing housing expenses, one must use this information.

Based on the rationale that over time the presence of a child in a home does not affect the number of kitchens or living rooms, but does affect the number of bedrooms (analysis of CE data confirmed this), the average cost of an additional bedroom approach was used to estimate housing expenses on a child in husband-wife and single-parent households. Previously, a per capita approach was used by USDA to estimate children's housing expenses, where housing expenses were assigned to household members in equal proportions. Because more data on housing characteristics have been made available in the CE survey over time, this average cost of an additional bedroom approach was developed. Specifically, this approach calculates child-rearing housing expenses as the extra housing costs associated with an additional bedroom in a home for families with children and in each income interval. Multivariate analysis was used to determine the average additional costs by regressing housing expenditures on the number of bedrooms in a home controlling for income level. The analysis was conducted separately for husband-wife and single-parent families. Housing expenses were adjusted to account for regional variation in the case of husband-wife families.

Because most families with children resided in a three- or four-bedroom home, housing expenses on a child were calculated as the average additional cost of one (but not both) of these bedrooms. It was assumed that children in a two-child family do not share a bedroom. With this method, housing expenses on a child include the costs of utilities and furniture associated with the additional bedroom. These expenses also do not vary by age of the child because costs due to the bedroom would not be expected to differ much by age.

The average cost of an additional bedroom approach is a conservative estimate of housing expenses on children because it does not account fully for the fact that some families pay more for housing to live in a community with good schools or other amenities for children. Part of this expense is captured in the cost of the additional bedroom, but parents may be spending more on their own housing to live in certain communities than they would without children. In addition, it is a conservative estimate because it does not account fully for parents' purchasing of a home with a larger yard, a playroom, or child-specific furnishings in other rooms of the home because of children in the household; however, data on these housing characteristics are limited.

A variation of the average cost of an additional bedroom approach that could account for these factors (better schools, larger yards, etc.) would be to compare the extra housing expenses due to an additional bedroom of couples with children with the expenses of couples without children. Initial estimates based on this variation resulted in slightly higher housing expenses on a child than reported here. This approach was ultimately not used because of difficulties in establishing a comparison group of childless families not composed of "empty nest" households at various income levels.

In addition, it is likely that younger couples without children buy larger houses in anticipation of having children. Comparing the expenditures of these couples with those of similar couples with children could lead to underestimates of housing expenditures on children because couples without children have incorporated possible future children in their housing expenditures. For single-parent households, selection of a comparison group is difficult. Single individuals (with no children) would include many people spending more on housing because they do not have child-rearing obligations. Using the housing expense difference between these people and single-parent families could lead to severe underestimates of housing expenditures on children in single-parent families.

For more information on how the USDA child-rearing housing expense estimates compare to alternative methodologies, including per capita and marginal cost approaches, and how they may be adjusted to reflect these alternative methodologies, see Lino and Carlson (2010).

Results

Complete estimates of child-rearing expenditures by husband-wife and single-parent families are contained in tables 1-7 at the end of this report. The following sections discuss major findings regarding these child-rearing expenditures.

Husband-Wife Families

Child-Rearing Expenses and Household Income Are Positively Related

In 2012, estimated annual average expenses on the younger child in two-child, husband-wife families increased as income level rose (figure 1). Depending on age of the child, annual expenses ranged from $8,990 to $10,230 for families with a before-tax income less than $60,640, from $12,600 to $14,700 for families with a before-tax income between $60,640 and $105,000, and from $20,930 to $25,180 for families with a before-tax income more than $105,000.

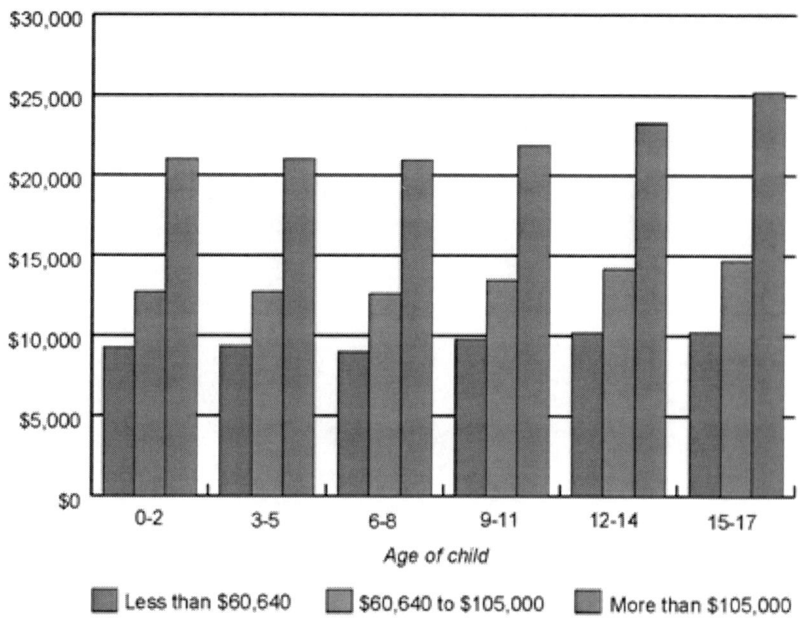

[1] U.S. average for the younger child in husband-wife families with two children.

Figure 1. Family expenditures on a child, by income level and age of child,[1] 2012.

On average, households in the lowest income group spent 25 percent of their before-tax income on a child; those in the middle-income group, 16 percent; and those in the highest group, 12 percent. The range among these percentages would be narrower if after-tax income were considered.

The amount spent on a child by families in the highest income group, on average, was more than twice the amount spent by families in the lowest income group. This amount varied by budgetary component. In general, expenses on a child for goods and services considered to be necessities (e.g., food and clothing) did not vary as much as those considered to be discretionary (e.g., miscellaneous expenses) among households in the three income groups.

Housing Is the Largest Expense on a Child

Housing accounted for the largest share of total child-rearing expenses. Figure 2 demonstrates this for the younger child in husband-wife, middle-income families with two children. Based on expenses incurred among all age groups, housing accounted for 32 percent of child-rearing expenses for a child in the lowest income group, 30 percent in the middle-income group, and 33 percent in the highest income group.

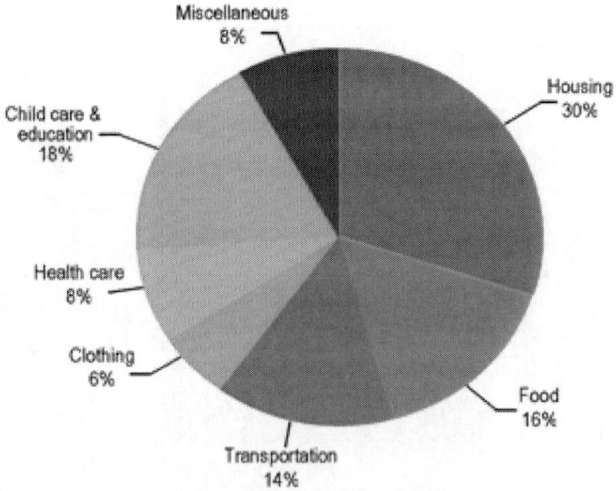

[1] U.S. average for the younger child in middle-income, husband-wife families with two children. Child care and education expenses only for families with expense.

Figure 2. Expenditure shares on a child from birth through age 17 as a percentage of total child-rearing expenditures, [1] 2012.

As previously discussed, child care and education was the only budgetary component for which many households had a zero expenditure and the others had a positive expenditure. The USDA estimates include only families with expenditures on this budgetary component. For the middle and highest income groups (for households with the expense), child care and education was the second largest expenditure on a child, accounting for 18 and 23 percent of child-rearing expenses, respectively. For the lowest income group, child care and education accounted for 14 percent of total child-rearing expenses (again, for households with the expense). It should be noted for lower income families, child care may be provided by relatives or friends at no cost due to affordability issues.

Food was the second largest expense on a child for families in the lowest income group, accounting for 18 percent of total expenditures. Food was the third largest expense on a child for families in the middle income group, accounting for 16 percent of total expenditures. Transportation made up 13 to 15 percent of total child-rearing expenses over the income groups.

Across the three income groups, miscellaneous goods and services accounted for 6 to 9 percent of child-rearing expenses; clothing (excluding gifts or hand-me-downs), 5 to 7 percent; and health care, 6 to 8 percent. Expenditures for health care consist of out-of-pocket expenses only (including insurance premiums not paid by an employer or other organizations) and not that portion covered by health insurance. Annual expenditures on clothing for teens, as based on the CE data, are similar to the findings of another survey of annual spending on teen apparel (PiperJaffray, 2011).

Expenses Increase as a Child Ages

Expenditures on a child in husband-wife families were generally lower in the younger age categories and higher in the older age categories. Figure 3 depicts this for families in the middle-income group. This relationship held across income groups. For all three income groups, food, transportation, clothing, and health care expenses on a child generally increased as the child grew older. As children age, they have greater nutritional needs so consume more food. Transportation expenses were highest for a child age 15 to 17, when he or she would start driving. Child care and education expenses were generally highest for a child under age 6. Most of this expense may be attributed to child care at this age.

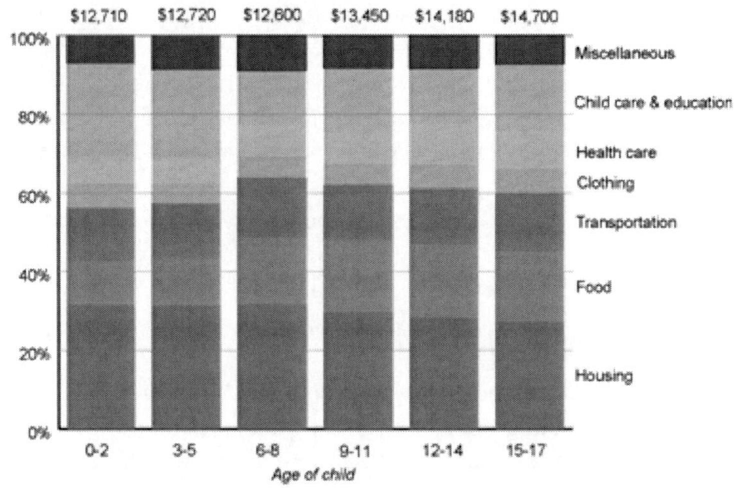

[1] U.S. average for the younger child in middle-income, husband-wife families with two children. Child care and education expenses only for families with expense.

Figure 3. Total expenses and expenditure shares on a child (as a percentage of total child-rearing expenditures), by age of child,1 2012.

Child-Rearing Expenses Are Highest in the Urban Northeast

Child-rearing expenses in the regions of the country reflect patterns observed in the overall United States for husband-wife families: In each region, expenses on a child increased with household income level and typically with age of the child. Figure 4 shows total child-rearing expenses by region and age of a child for the younger child in middle-income, two-child families. Overall, child-rearing expenses were highest in the urban Northeast, followed by the urban West and urban Midwest. Child-rearing expenses were lowest in the urban South and rural areas. Much of the regional difference in expenses on a child was related to housing costs and child care and education expenses. Total housing expenses on a child were highest in the urban Northeast and urban West and lowest in rural areas. Child care and education expenses were highest for families in the urban Northeast. Child-rearing transportation expenses were highest for families in the urban West and rural areas. This likely reflects the longer traveling distances in these areas.

Single-Parent Families

Expenses on a child in single-parent families generally followed the same pattern as expenses on a child in husband-wife families: Expenses increased as household income level rose; housing, food, and child care/education (for those with the expense) accounted for the largest budgetary shares; and more was spent as children aged. An interesting question is, "How do child-rearing expenses of single-parent families compare with those of husband-wife families?"

Figure 5 presents a comparison of estimated expenditures on a younger child in a two-child, husband-wife and single-parent household with a before-tax income less than $60,640; as previously discussed, 85 percent of single-parent families and 33 percent of husband-wife families were in this lower income group and this income included child support payments. Total expenditures on a child up to age 18 were, on average, 7 percent lower in single-parent households than in husband-wife households. But more single-parent than husband-wife families were in the bottom range of this income group. Average income for single-parent families in the lower income group was $26,900, compared with $38,790 for husband-wife families. Because single-parent families have one less potential earner, their total household income is lower and child-rearing expenses consume a greater percentage of income.

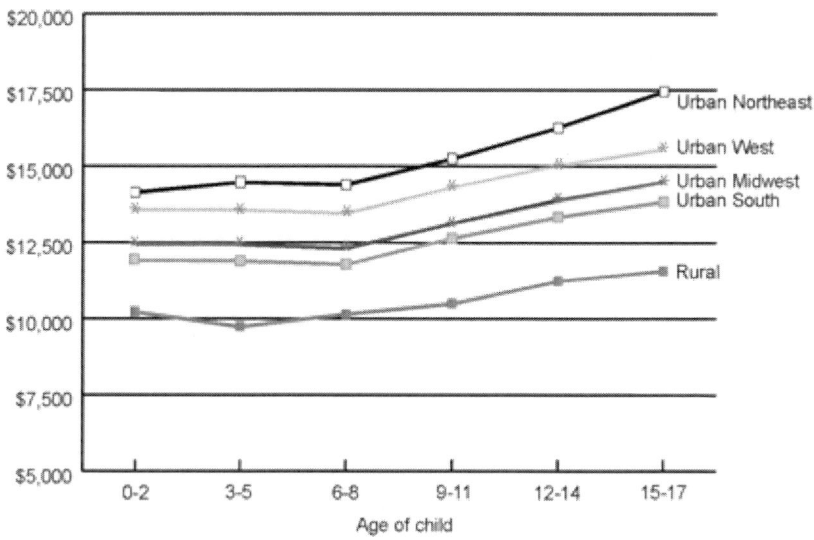

[1] Regional averages for the younger child in middle-income, husband-wife families with two children.

Figure 4. Family expenditures on a child, by region and age of child,1 2012.

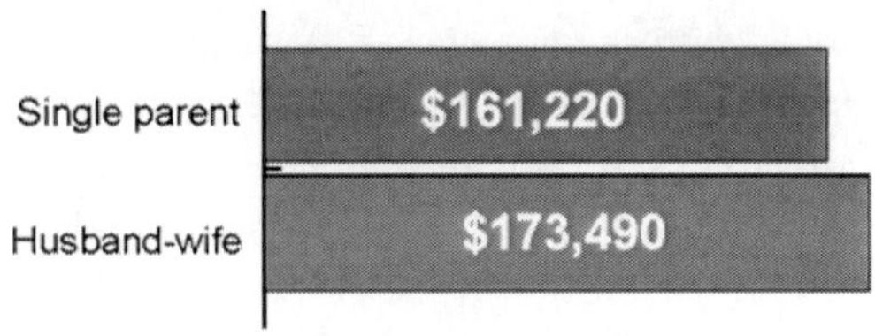

[1] U.S. average for the younger child in two-child families with before-tax income below $60,640.

Figure 5. Family expenditures on a child from birth to age 18, by single-parent and husband-wife households, 1 in 2012 dollars.

For single parents, the estimates only cover out-of-pocket child-rearing expenditures made by the parent who has primary care of the child. The estimates do not include child-related expenditures made by the parent without primary care or by others, such as grandparents. The parent with whom the child does not reside the majority of the time may incur transportation, food, and entertainment expenses during visitation days and maintain a larger living unit because the child stays with him or her on weekends. The noncustodial parent could also contribute to the child's clothing and health care expenses. Although it would be ideal to include these expenditures, such expenditures could not be estimated from the CE data. Overall expenses paid by both parents on a child in a single-parent household, therefore, are likely to be greater than this study's estimates.

Adjustments for Older Children and Household Size

The estimates of expenses on children thus far represent expenditures on the younger child in a husband-wife and single-parent household with two children. Expenses on the older child may be different for the two family types. To determine the extent of this difference and how expenditures may be adjusted to estimate expenses on an older child, the USDA methodology to estimate expenditures on children was essentially repeated with the focus on an older child in each family type. Household income and region of residence (in the case of husband-wife households) were not controlled for, so findings apply to all families. The sample was smaller than that used for the principal analysis, since only households with all children age 17 or under were selected because the older child could not be over this age. The sample was weighted to reflect the U.S. population of interest.

It was found that the data in tables 1-6 (pp. 26-31) reflect total expenditures on an older child in a husband-wife, two-child family, as well as on a younger child. Therefore, annual expenditures on children in a husband-wife, two-child family may be estimated by summing the total expenses for the specific age categories of the two children. For example, annual expenditures on a younger child age 11 and an older child age 16 in a husband-wife, two-child family in the middle-income group for the overall United States would be $28,150 (= $13,450 + $14,700) (table 8).

Table 8. Estimated annual expenditures on one, two, or three children by husband-wife and single-parent families, overall United States, 2012

Husband-wife family*		
One-child household		
Age of child		**Annual expenditure**
2		$12,710 x 1.25 = $15,890
5		12,720 x 1.25 = 15,900
8		12,600 x 1.25 = 15,750
11		13,450 x 1.25 = 16,810
14		14,180 x 1.25 = 17,730
17		14,700 x 1.25 = 18,380
Two-child household		
Age of younger child	**Age of older child**	
2	16	$12,710 + $14,700 = $27,410
5	16	12,720 + 14,700 = 27,420
8	16	12,600 + 14,700 = 27,300
11	16	13,450 + 14,700 = 28,150
14	16	14,180 + 14,700 = 28,880
15	16	14,700 + 14,700 = 29,400
Three-child household		
Age of youngest child	**Age of older children**	
2	13,16	($12,710 + $14,180 + $14,700) x .78 = $32,440
5	13,16	(12,720 + 14,180 + 14,700) x .78 = 32,450
8	13,16	(12,600 + 14,180 + 14,700) x .78 = 32,350
11	13,16	(13,450 + 14,180 + 14,700) x .78 = 33,020
12	13,16	(14,180 + 14,180 + 14,700) x .78 = 33,590

Table 8. (Continued)

Single-parent family**		
One-child household		
Age of child		**Annual expenditure**
2		$7,950 x 1.29 = $10,260
5		8,830 x 1.29 = 11,390
8		8,660 x 1.29 = 11,170
11		9,250 x 1.29 = 11,930
14		9,660 x 1.29 = 12,460
17		9,390 x 1.29 = 12,110
Two-child household		
Age of younger child	**Age of older child**	
2	16	$7,950 + ($9,390 x .97) = $17,060
5	16	8,830 + (9,390 x .97) = 17,940
8	16	8,660 + (9,390 x .97) = 17,770
11	16	9,250 + (9,390 x .97) = 18,360
14	16	9,660 + (9,390 x .97) = 18,770
15	16	9,390 + (9,390 x .97) = 18,500
Three-child household		
Age of youngest child	**Age of older children**	
2	13,16	($7,950 + ($9,660 x .97) + ($9,390 x .97)) x .77 = $20,350
5	13,16	(8,830 + (9,660 x .97) + (9,390 x .97)) x .77 = 21,030
8	13,16	(8,660 + (9,660 x .97) + (9,390 x .97)) x .77 = 20,900
11	13,16	(9,250 + (9,660 x .97) + (9,390 x .97)) x .77 = 21,350
12	13,16	(9,660 + (9,660 x .97) + (9,390 x .97)) x .77 = 21,670

* Estimates are for husband-wife families with 2012 before-tax income between $60,640 and $105,000.

** Estimates are for single-parent families with 2012 before-tax income less than $60,640.

Unlike husband-wife families, single-parent households with two children spend about 3 percent less on the older child than on the younger child at a specific age category. This reduced spending was largely due to less being spent on transportation and miscellaneous goods and services for the older child. Older children in single-parent families may be able to take less expensive public transportation rather than be driven by the parent in a car and forgo some items that the younger child has received. Also, some of these expenses may be covered by others not residing in the home. Therefore, annual expenditures on children in a single-parent, two-child family may be estimated from table 7 (p. 32) by: (1) taking the age category of the older child and adjusting the total expenses downward by 3 percent, and then (2) summing the total expenses for the specific age categories of the two children. For example, annual expenditures on a younger child age 8 and an older child age 16 in a single-parent, two-child family in the lower income group for the overall United States would be $17,770 (= $8,660 + ($9,390 X .97)) (table 8). It should be noted that for specific budgetary components, annual expenses on an older child in husband-wife and single-parent families varied, compared with those on a younger child in a two-child family.

The estimates should also be adjusted if a household has only one child or more than two children. Families will spend more or less on a child, depending on the number of other children in the household (income being spread over fewer or more children) and as a result of economies of scale. To derive these adjustments, the USDA methodology to estimate expenditures on children was replicated for both husband-wife and single-parent families with one child and three or more children. The maximum number of children was restricted to three or more because only a small percentage of families had four or more children.

Household income and region of residence (in the case of husband-wife households) were not controlled for, so findings apply to all families. For families with three or more children, the possibility of children sharing a bedroom was factored in by examining the number of bedrooms and number of children in the household.

Compared with expenditures for each child in a husband-wife, two-child family, husband-wife households with one child spend an average of 25 percent more on the single child, and those with three or more children spend an average of 22 percent less on each child. For single- parent families, those with one child spend an average of 29 percent more on the single child than on a child in a two-child family, and those with three or more children spend an average of 23 percent less on each child. As families have more children, the children can share a bedroom, clothing and toys can be handed down to younger children, food can be purchased in larger and more economical packages, and private schools or child care centers may offer sibling discounts.

Therefore, to estimate annual overall expenditures on an only child by using data in tables 1-7, 25 percent should be added to the total expense for each age category for husband-wife families and 29 percent should be added to the total expense for each age category for single-parent families. To estimate expenses on three or more children in husband-wife families, 22 percent should be subtracted from the total expense for each child's age category and these totals should be summed. For single-parent families with three or more children, 23 percent should be subtracted from the total expense for each child's age category (after adjusting the expenses on the older children downward), and these totals should be summed. These percentages may be more or less for a particular budgetary component for both family types. As family size increases, costs per child for food decrease less than for housing and transportation. Much housing space is used in common, and car trips can serve more than one child.

As an example of adjustments needed for different numbers of children, consider total expenses on children in husband-wife families with one, two, and three children (presented in table 8 for a household with before-tax income between \$60,640 and \$105,000). In the example, the age of the older child is 16 in the two-child household and the ages of the older children are 13 and 16 in the three-child household. As can be seen, less is spent per child as family size increases. The estimated annual expense on a child age 2 with no siblings is \$15,890; for two children ages 2 and 16, \$27,410; and for three children ages 2, 13, and 16, \$32,440. Table 8 also shows the expenditure adjustments needed for children in single-parent families with one, two, and three children and with a before-tax income below \$60,640. The major difference in the mechanics of the adjustment for single-parent, compared with husband-wife households, is that the expenses on older children need to be adjusted downward by 3 percent.

Alternative Estimates of Expenditures on Children

The USDA methodology to estimate child-rearing expenses is based on several steps: (1) assigning child-specific expenses (clothing, child care, and education) in the CE data to children, (2) allocating household-level expenses based on findings from authoritative research (food and health care) or on a per capita basis (transportation and miscellaneous items), and (3) calculating housing expenses by using an approach that accounts for the average cost of an additional bedroom. An alternative method to estimate expenditures on children is a marginal cost method. The marginal cost method measures expenditures on children as the difference in expenses between families with children and equivalent families without children. While there is no generally accepted equivalency measure in the economics literature, two of the most commonly used are the Engel and Rothbarth approaches. The Engel approach assumes that if two families spend an equal percentage of their total expenditures on food, they are equally well-off. The Rothbarth approach assumes that if two families spend an equal amount on luxuries (e.g., alcohol, tobacco, entertainment, and sweets) and have the same level of savings, they are equally well-off. (See U.S. Department of Health and Human Services, 1990, for more detailed information on these two approaches.)

One limitation of the Engel and Rothbarth estimators is that they are not true marginal cost approaches. A true marginal cost approach examines additional expenditures a family makes because of the presence of a child in the household—how much more the family spends on housing, food, and other items because of the child. A true marginal cost approach would track the same sample of families over time. Marginal cost approaches, as implemented, do not do this. They examine two different sets of families, those with children and those without children, at one point in time. Hence, the term "marginal cost approach" is somewhat of a misnomer.

Another limitation with the marginal cost approach is that it does not consider substitution effects. It assumes parents do not alter their expenditures on themselves after a child is added to a household. This could lead to problems when applying the marginal cost method to individual budgetary components. For example, many families may reduce the number of high-cost vacations they take once they have children. However, with the marginal cost method, transportation expenses of these families without children would be compared with expenses of families with children, likely leading to underestimates of transportation expenses on a child.

These problems with the marginal cost method are likely more severe if used to calculate miscellaneous expenses on a child. Published data show entertainment expenses, one of the major components of the miscellaneous category, were greater for husband-wife couples without children than for husband-wife families with young children (U.S. Department of Labor, 2008). Using the marginal cost method in this case could lead to the questionable result of having negative entertainment expenditures on a child. The household entertainment expenses of husband-wife couples without children were about the same as those of husband- wife families with an oldest child over age 18 living in the household, suggesting a miniscule expenditure on a child (U.S. Department of Labor, 2008).

Since 2000, several studies have estimated child-rearing expenses by using both the Engel and Rothbarth estimators and applying them to Consumer Expenditure Survey data. Table 9 shows the child-rearing expense estimates produced by these studies for husband-wife families by number of children and as a percentage of total family expenditures; these studies estimated child-rearing expenses as a percentage of total expenditures and did not examine expenses by budgetary component. It should be noted that the Rothbarth method was usually implemented by using only adult clothing as the equivalency method so is not a full implementation of the Rothbarth approach. Hence, how results would differ if a more complete Rothbarth approach were implemented is unknown. An earlier study found the results of the Rothbarth approach to vary considerably depending on the budgetary items included in the equivalency scale definition and concluded this revealed a significant weakness in the practical application of the approach (Lancaster and Ray, 1998).

What is striking is the range in estimates resulting from the various studies. For one child, the estimates ranged between 21 to 32 percent of household expenditures being spent on the child; for two children, 31 to 47 percent; and for three children, 38 to 57 percent (almost a 20-percentage- point difference). When using the marginal cost method in estimating expenditures on children, a researcher's choice of an equivalency scale is crucial because different measures yield different results. Even using the same equivalency measure can result in different estimates, depending on the years of data used and model specification. For example, the 2011 study based on the Rothbarth estimator found that for two-child families, 37 percent of total family expenditures went to goods and services for children (Judicial Council of California, 2011), while the 2008 study using the Rothbarth estimator found that 47 percent of expenditures went to goods and services for two children (McCaleb et al., 2008). The 2008 study found the Rothbarth estimator to be the most sensitive to underlying data and sample restrictions. Also, the 2011 study calls into question the validity of the Engel approach.

So, how do the USDA child-rearing expense estimates compare with the results of these studies? Table 9 presents the USDA (2013) estimates. Because the studies implementing the Engel and Rothbarth techniques usually did not include personal insurance and pension contributions in total household expenditures, when calculating the USDA child-rearing expenses as a percentage of total household expenditures, these two budgetary components were not included. Also, the marginal cost methods include families with child care/education expenses and families without child care/education expenses and many do not include mortgage principal payments, so the USDA estimates in table 9 are based on average child care/education expenses for all husband-wife families, including those without the expense, and do not include mortgage principal, which constitutes about 15 percent of overall housing expenses. This differs from the USDA child-rearing expenditure estimates in tables 1-7, where mortgage principal payments are included in housing expenses and where child care/education expenses are only for families incurring the expense. If mortgage principal was included, the USDA estimates on table 9 would be 1 percentage point higher for one-child families (28 percent) and 2 percentage points higher for two- and three-children families (43 and 49 percent).

For husband-wife families with one child, USDA estimates 27 percent of total family expenditures are spent on the child; for two children, 41 percent; and for three children, 47 percent. These percentages are very near the averages of the various studies using the Engel and Rothbarth approaches. One factor the various approaches have in common is that expenditures on children do not increase proportionately as the number of children increases; expenditures on two children are less than twice as much as those on one child.

Table 9. Average percent of household expenditures attributable to children in husband-wife families, by estimator and number of children

Number of children	**One**	**Two**	**Three**
	Percent		
Estimator			
Engel (2001)[1]	30	44	52
Rothbarth (2001)[1]	26	36	42
Rothbarth (2006)[2]	25	37	44
Engel (2008)[3]	21	31	38
Rothbarth (2008)[3]	32	47	57
Rothbarth (2011)[4]	24	37	45
Average of above	26	39	46
USDA (2013)	27	41	47

[1] From Judicial Council of California (2001).
[2] From Policy Studies Inc. (2006).
[3] From McCaleb, Macpherson, and Norrbin (2008).
[4] From Judicial Council of California (2011).

Table 10. Estimated annual expenditures* on a child born in 2012 by income group, overall United States

Year	Age	Income Group		
		Lowest	Middle	Highest
2012	<1	$9,290	$12,710	$21,000
2013	1	9,520	13,030	21,530
2014	2	9,760	13,350	22,060
2015	3	10,060	13,700	22,610
2016	4	10,310	14,040	23,180
2017	5	10,570	14,390	23,760
2018	6	10,430	14,610	24,270
2019	7	10,690	14,980	24,880
2020	8	10,950	15,350	25,500
2021	9	12,210	16,800	27,310
2022	10	12,520	17,220	28,000
2023	11	12,830	17,650	28,700
2024	12	13,720	19,070	31,310
2025	13	14,060	19,550	32,090
2026	14	14,410	20,040	32,890
2027	15	14,820	21,290	36,470
2028	16	15,190	21,820	37,380
2029	17	15,570	22,370	38,310
Total		**$216,910**	**$301,970**	**$501,250**

* Estimates are for the younger child in husband-wife families with two children and assume an average annual inflation rate of 2.5 percent.

Estimating Future Costs

The estimates presented so far represent household expenditures on a child of a certain age in 2012. What would be the total expenses on a child born in 2012 through age 17, factoring in inflation? To estimate these expenses over time, future price changes need to be incorporated. To do this, a future cost formula is used:

$$C_f = C_p (1 + i)^n$$

Where:

C_f = projected future annual dollar expenditure on a child of a particular age

C_p = present (2012) annual dollar expenditure on a child of a particular age

i = projected annual inflation (or deflation) rate

n = number of years from present until child will reach a particular age

An example of estimated future expenditures on the younger child in a husband-wife family with two children is presented in table 10. The example assumes a child is born in 2012 and reaches age 17 in the year 2029, and the average annual inflation rate over this time is 2.5 percent (the average annual inflation rate over the past 20 years) (U.S. Department of Labor, 2013). As can be seen, total family expenses on a child through age 17 would be $216,910 for households in the lowest income group, $301,970 for those in the middle, and $501,250 for those in the highest income group. In 2012 dollar values, these figures would be $173,490, $241,080, and $399,780, respectively.

Inflation rates other than 2.5 percent could be used in the formula if inflation projections change. Also, it is somewhat unrealistic to assume that households remain in one income category as a child grows older. For most families, income rises over time, so a family may move from one income group to another. In addition, such inflation projections assume child- rearing expenditures change only with inflation. Parental expenditure patterns also change over time.

Expenditures Not Included

Expenditures estimated in this study consisted of direct parental expenses made on children through age 17 for seven major budgetary components. These expenditures exclude costs related to prenatal health care. The expenditures also exclude costs made on children after age 17. One of the largest of these excluded expenses is the cost of a college education. The College Board (2013) estimated that in 2012-2013, annual average (enrollment-weighted) tuition and fees were $8,655 at 4-year public colleges (in-State tuition) and $29,056 at 4-year private (non-profit) colleges; annual room and board was $9,205 at 4-year public colleges and $10,462 at 4-year private colleges. For 2-year colleges in 2012-2013, annual average tuition and fees were $3,131 at public colleges. These college costs may be offset by financial aid. College-related expenses on children may even take place before children are college age in the form of savings. Other parental expenses on children after age 17 could include those associated with children living at home or if children do not live at home, gifts and other contributions to them. Expenses related to life insurance on parents are not included in the estimates. Although these expenses are not made directly on children, it is likely that they are primarily incurred for the benefit of children.

EXPENDITURES ON CHILDREN: 1960 VERSUS 2012

The U.S. Department of Agriculture first provided estimates of child-rearing expenditures in 1960. The current estimates are not precisely comparable to previous estimates because of methodology changes; for example, housing expenses are now determined by using the average cost of an additional bedroom as opposed to a per capita approach, and food expenses are now based on what households spend as opposed to a suggested standard. Although these types of methodological changes exist, a general comparison is possible.

In 1960, average expenditures on a child in a middle-income, husband-wife family amounted to $25,229, or $195,690 in 2012 dollars (figure). By 2012, these estimated expenditures climbed 23 percent in real terms to $241,080 (assuming a family had child care and education expenses on a child). Housing was the largest expense on a child in both time periods and increased in real terms over this time. Food was also one of the largest expenses in both time periods, but decreased in real terms. Changes in agriculture over the past 50 years have resulted in family food budgets being a lower percentage of household income. Transportation expenses on a child increased slightly in real terms from 1960 to 2012.

Clothing and miscellaneous expenses on a child decreased as a percentage of total child-rearing expenses and in real terms from 1960 to 2012. Reduced real expenses on children's clothing is somewhat of a surprise given the popularity of many designer clothing items today; however, it is likely that technological changes and globalization have made clothing less expensive in real terms. The growth in real terms of housing and other expenses on a child may be the cause of the decline in miscellaneous expenses on a child, which are often seen as discretionary.

Health care expenses on a child doubled as a percentage of total child-rearing costs, as well as increasing in real terms, from 1960 to 2012. The dramatic rise in health care costs over time has received widespread attention.

Perhaps the most striking change in child- rearing expenses over time relates to child care and education expenses. It should be noted that in 1960, child care/education expenses included families with and without the expense. Even so, these expenses grew from 2 percent of total child-rearing expenditures in 1960 (for families with and without the expense) to 18 percent (for families with the expense) in 2012. Much of this growth is likely related to child care. In 1960, child care costs were negligible, mainly consisting of in-the-home babysitting. Since then, the labor force participation of women has greatly increased, leading to the need for more child care. Child-rearing expense estimates were not provided for single-parent families in 1960, likely because of the small percentage of children residing in such households at the time.

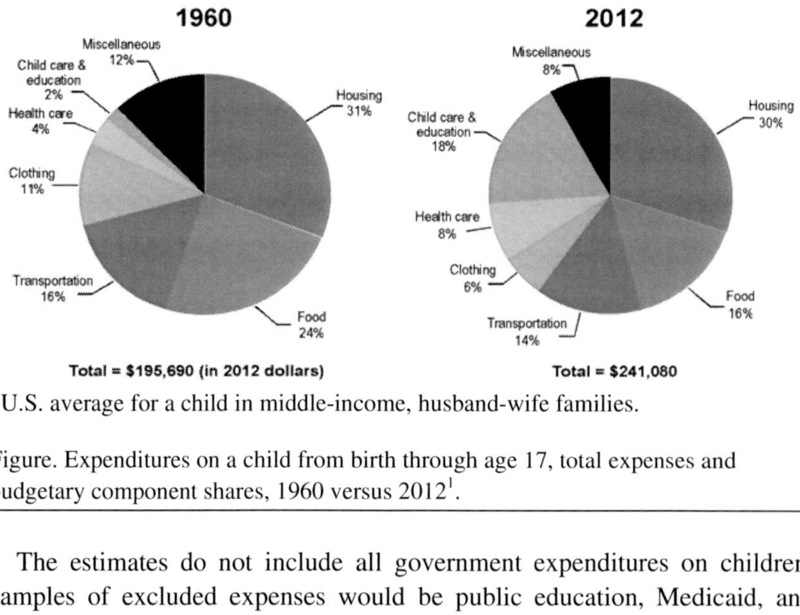

[1] U.S. average for a child in middle-income, husband-wife families.

Figure. Expenditures on a child from birth through age 17, total expenses and budgetary component shares, 1960 versus 2012[1].

The estimates do not include all government expenditures on children. Examples of excluded expenses would be public education, Medicaid, and subsidized school meals. The actual expenditures on children (by parents and the government), therefore, would be higher than reported in this study, especially for children in the lowest income group. Expenditures on children made by people not in the household, such as grandparents and other relatives, were also not factored in the estimates. Indirect costs involved in child rearing were not included in the estimates. Although these costs are typically more difficult to measure than direct expenditures, they may be substantial. The time involved in rearing children is considerable and has a cost attached to it.

One study found that the imputed value of parental time spent on children exceeded the direct cash expenditures on them (Folbre, 2008). In addition, to care for children, current earnings and future career opportunities may be diminished because of job choice or reduced time in the labor force for one or both parents. These situations also have a cost attached to them.

The direct and indirect costs of raising children are considerable, absorbing a major share of the household budget. On the other hand, these costs may be outweighed by the benefits of children.

REFERENCES

Bernard, D. (2007). *Out-of-Pocket Expenditures on Health Care Among the Nonelderly Population, 2004.* (Statistical Brief #159). Agency for Healthcare Research and Quality, Rockville, MD: Department of Health and Human Services.

Dublin, L. I. & Lotka, A. J. (1946). *The Money Value of a Man.* New York City, NY: Ronald Press.

Folbre, N. (2008). *Valuing Children: Rethinking the Economics of the Family.* Cambridge, MA: Harvard University Press.

The College Board. (2013). *Trends in College Pricing 2012.* Retrieved March 15, 2013, from http://trends.collegeboard.org/sites/default/files/college-pricing-2012-full-report_0.pdf.

Hu, P. S & Reuscher, T. R. (2004). *Summary of Travel Trends: 2001 National Household Travel Survey.* Washington, DC: U.S. Department of Transportation, Federal Highway Administration.

Judicial Council of California. (2001). *Review of Statewide Uniform Child Support Guideline*. Retrieved March 27, 2009 at http://www.courtinfo.ca.gov/programs/cfcc/pdffiles/ChildSupport- 2001UniformChildSupport Guideline.pdf.

Judicial Council of California. (2011). *Review of Statewide Uniform Child Support Guideline 2010.* Retrieved March 14, 2012, from http://www.courts.ca.gov/documents/review-sucsg-0611.pdf.

Lancaster, G. & Ray, R. (1998). Comparison of alternative models of household equivalence scales: The Australian evidence on unit record data. *The Economic Record*, *74*(224), 1-14.

Lino, M. & Carlson, A. (2010). Estimating housing expenses on children: A comparison of methodologies. *Journal of Legal Economics*, *16*(2), 61-79.

Lino, M. (2008). *Expenditures on Children by Families, 2007.* U.S. Department of Agriculture, Center for Nutrition Policy and Promotion. (Miscellaneous Publication Number 1528-2007).

McCaleb, T.S., Macpherson, D.A., & Norrbin, S.C. (2008). *Review and Update of Florida's Child Support Guidelines.* Report to the Florida Legislature, November17, 2008.

McDonald, J. F. & Moffitt, R. A. (1980). The uses of Tobit analysis. *The Review of Economics and Statistics*, *62*(2), 318-321.

PiperJaffray. (2011). *Taking Stock With Teens, Spring 2011.* Retrieved March 8, 2013, from http://jettnermarketing.files.wordpress.com/2011/10/spring-2011-taking-stock-with-teens.pdf.

Policy Studies Inc. (Venohr, J., Betson, D., Price, D., Zoller, M., & Washington, L.) (2006). *State of Oregon Child Support Guidelines Review: Updated Obligation Scales and Other Considerations.* Submitted to Department of Justice, Division of Child Support on June 26, 2006.

U.S. Census Bureau. (2011). Who's Minding the Kids? Child Care Arrangements: Spring 2010—Detailed Tables. Retrieved March 7, 2012, from http://www.census.gov/hhes/childcare/ data/sipp/2010/tables.html.

U.S. Department of Agriculture, Agricultural Research Service. (1981). *USDA Estimates of the Cost of Raising a Child: A Guide to Their Use and Interpretation.* (Miscellaneous Publication No. 1411).

U.S. Department of Agriculture, Center for Nutrition Policy and Promotion. (2008). *Official USDA Food Plans: Cost of Food at Home at Four Levels, U.S. Average, March 2008.* Alexandria, VA.

U.S. Department of Health and Human Services, Office of the Assistant Secretary for Planning and Evaluation. (1990). *Estimates of Expenditures on Children and Child Support Guidelines.*

U.S. Department of Labor, Bureau of Labor Statistics. (2007). *2005 Consumer Expenditure Interview Survey Public Use Microdata Documentation.*

U.S. Department of Labor, Bureau of Labor Statistics. (2008). *Composition of Consumer Unit: Average Annual Expenditures and Characteristics, Consumer Expenditure Survey, 2006.* Retrieved November 5, 2008, from http://www.bls.gov/cex/2006/Standard/cucomp.pdf.

U.S. Department of Labor, Bureau of Labor Statistics. (2013). *Consumer Price Index.* Retrieved March 15, 2013, from ftp://ftp.bls.gov/pub/special. requests/cpi/cpiai.txt.

In: Cost of Raising a Child
Editor: Athena M. Byers

ISBN: 978-1-62948-369-6

Chapter 2

EXPENDITURES ON CHILDREN BY FAMILIES, 2011*

Mark Lino

ABSTRACT

Since 1960, the U.S. Department of Agriculture has provided estimates of expenditures on children from birth through age 17. This technical report presents the most recent estimates for husband-wife and single-parent families using data from the 2005-06 Consumer Expenditure Survey, updated to 2011 dollars using the Consumer Price Index. Data and methods used in calculating annual child-rearing expenses are described. Estimates are provided for major components of the budget by age of child, family income, and region of residence. For the overall United States, annual child-rearing expense estimates ranged between $12,290 and $14,320 for a child in a two-child, married-couple family in the middle-income group. Adjustment factors for number of children in the household are also provided. Results of this study should be of use in developing State child support and foster care guidelines, as well as in family educational programs.

* This is an edited, reformatted and augmented version of the U.S. Department of Agriculture, Center for Nutrition Policy and Promotion, Miscellaneous Publication No. 1528-2011, dated June, 2012.

EXECUTIVE SUMMARY

Since 1960, the U.S Department of Agriculture (USDA) has provided estimates of annual expenditures on children from birth through age 17. This technical report presents the 2011 estimates for husband-wife and single-parent families. Results are shown in tables 1-7 at the end of this report. Expenditures are provided by age of children, household income level, major budgetary component (housing, food, etc.), and region (for husband-wife families).

Methods

Data used to estimate expenditures on children are from the 2005-06 Consumer Expenditure Survey—Interview portion (CE). Administered by the U.S. Census Bureau, U.S. Department of Commerce, under contract with the Bureau of Labor Statistics (BLS), U.S. Department of Labor, this survey is the most comprehensive source of information on household expenditures available at the national level. The sample consisted of 11,800 husband-wife households and 3,350 single-parent households and was weighted to reflect the U.S. population of interest by using BLS weighting methods.

The CE collects overall household expenditure data for some budgetary components (housing, food, transportation, health care, and miscellaneous goods and services) and child-specific expenditure data for other components (clothing, child care, and education). Child-specific expenses were allocated directly to children. Food and health care expenses were allocated to children based on findings from Federal surveys on children's budget shares. Family-related transportation expenses and miscellaneous expenses were allocated by using a per capita method. This method is preferable over a marginal cost method that measures child-rearing expenditures as the difference in expenses between equivalent couples with and without children. The average cost of an additional bedroom approach was used to estimate housing expenses on a child.

Although based on the 2005-06 CE, the expense estimates were updated to 2011 dollars by using the Consumer Price Index (CPI) for specific budgetary components: 2005 expenditure and income data were first converted to 2006 dollars to complete the analysis and then the results were updated to 2011 dollars.

Table 1. Estimated annual expenditures on a child by husband-wife families, overall United States, 2012

Age of child	Total expense	Housing	Food	Transportation	Clothing	Health care	Child care and education[a]	Miscellaneous[b]
Before tax income: Less than $59,410 (Average = $38,000)								
0 - 2	$9,050	$2,990	$1,160	$1,170	$640	$630	$2,040	$420
3 - 5	9,100	2,990	1,260	1,230	500	590	1,910	620
6 - 8	8,760	2,990	1,710	1,350	570	660	850	630
9 - 11	9,520	2,990	1,970	1,350	580	710	1,290	630
12 - 14	9,960	2,990	2,130	1,480	690	1,090	880	700
15 - 17	9,970	2,990	2,120	1,630	730	1,010	910	580
Total	**$169,080**	**$53,820**	**$31,050**	**$24,630**	**$11,130**	**$14,070**	**$23,640**	**$10,740**
Before-tax income: $59,410 to $102,870 (Average = $79,940)								
0 - 2	$12,370	$3,920	$1,400	$1,690	$760	$850	$2,860	$890
3 - 5	12,390	3,920	1,490	1,740	610	800	2,740	1,090
6 - 8	12,290	3,920	2,100	1,860	680	940	1,680	1,110
9 - 11	13,110	3,920	2,400	1,870	710	1,000	2,110	1,100
12 - 14	13,820	3,920	2,580	1,990	840	1,410	1,910	1,170
15 - 17	14,320	3,920	2,570	2,150	900	1,330	2,400	1,050
Total	**$234,900**	**$70,560**	**$37,620**	**$33,900**	**$13,500**	**$18,990**	**$41,100**	**$19,230**
Before-tax income: More than $102,870 (Average = $180,040)								
0 - 2	$20,460	$7,100	$1,900	$2,550	$1,050	$980	$5,090	$1,790
3 - 5	20,480	7,100	2,000	2,610	880	930	4,970	1,990
6 - 8	20,420	7,100	2,630	2,730	970	1,080	3,910	2,000
9 - 11	21,320	7,100	2,980	2,730	1,010	1,150	4,350	2,000
12 - 14	22,700	7,100	3,190	2,860	1,170	1,610	4,700	2,070

Table 1. (Continued)

Age of child	Total expense	Housing	Food	Transportation	Clothing	Health care	Child care and education[a]	Miscellaneous[b]
15 - 17	24,510	7,100	3,180	3,020	1,280	1,520	6,460	1,950
Total	**$389,670**	**$127,800**	**$47,640**	**$49,500**	**$19,080**	**$21,810**	**$88,440**	**$35,400**

Estimates are based on 2005-06 Consumer Expenditure Survey data updated to 2011 dollars by using the Consumer Price Index. For each age category, the expense estimates represent average child-rearing expenditures for each age (e.g., the expense for the 3-5 age category, on average, applies to the 3-year-old, the 4-year-old, or the 5-year-old). The Total (0 - 17) row represents the expenditure sum of all ages (0, 1, 2, 3,...17) in 2011 dollars. The figures represent estimated expenses on the younger child in a two-child family. Estimates are about the same for the older child, so to calculate expenses for two children, figures should be summed for the appropriate age categories. To estimate expenses for an only child, multiply the total expense for the appropriate age category by 1.25. To estimate expenses for each child in a family with three or more children, multiply the total expense for each appropriate age category by 0.78.

For expenses on all children in a family, these totals should be summed.

[a] Includes only families with child care and education expenses.

[b] Includes personal care items, entertainment, and reading materials.

Table 2. Estimated annual expenditures on a child by husband-wife families, urban Northeast, 2011

Age of child	Total expense	Housing	Food	Transportation	Clothing	Health care	Child care and education[a]	Miscellaneous[b]
Before-tax income: Less than $59,690 (Average = $38,180)								
0 - 2	$10,740	$3,570	$1,230	$1,110	$720	$560	$3,120	$430
3 - 5	10,760	3,570	1,340	1,160	570	530	2,950	640
6 - 8	10,460	3,570	1,810	1,290	640	590	1,900	660

Age of child	Total expense	Housing	Food	Transportation	Clothing	Health care	Child care and education[a]	Miscellaneous[b]
9 - 11	11,210	3,570	2,080	1,290	660	640	2,320	650
12 - 14	11,930	3,570	2,250	1,420	790	970	2,210	720
15 - 17	12,650	3,570	2,250	1,570	850	900	2,910	600
Total	**$203,250**	**$64,260**	**$32,880**	**$23,520**	**$12,690**	**$12,570**	**$46,230**	**$11,100**
Before-tax income: $59,690 to $103,350 (Average = $80,310)								
0 - 2	$14,150	$4,680	$1,470	$1,630	$850	$770	$3,850	$900
3 - 5	14,110	4,680	1,560	1,690	680	720	3,680	1,100
6 - 8	14,050	4,680	2,190	1,820	770	850	2,620	1,120
9 - 11	14,880	4,680	2,510	1,820	800	910	3,040	1,120
12 - 14	15,850	4,680	2,690	1,940	960	1,280	3,110	1,190
15 - 17	17,010	4,680	2,690	2,100	1,040	1,200	4,230	1,070
Total	**$270,150**	**$84,240**	**$39,330**	**$33,000**	**$15,300**	**$17,190**	**$61,590**	**$19,500**
Before-tax income: More than $103,350 (Average = $180,870)								
0 - 2	$22,800	$8,480	$1,960	$2,500	$1,150	$890	$6,030	$1,790
3 - 5	22,780	8,480	2,060	2,560	970	850	5,860	2,000
6 - 8	22,760	8,480	2,710	2,690	1,060	990	4,810	2,020
9 - 11	23,650	8,480	3,080	2,690	1,110	1,050	5,230	2,010
12 - 14	25,300	8,480	3,290	2,810	1,310	1,480	5,850	2,080
15 - 17	27,720	8,480	3,280	2,970	1,440	1,390	8,200	1,960
Total	**$435,030**	**$152,640**	**$49,140**	**$48,660**	**$21,120**	**$19,950**	**$107,940**	**$35,580**

Estimates are based on 2005-06 Consumer Expenditure Survey data updated to 2011 dollars by using the regional Consumer Price Index. For each age category, the expense estimates represent average child-rearing expenditures for each age (e.g., the expense for the 3-5 age category, on average, applies to the 3-year-old, the 4-year-old, or the 5-year-old). The Total (0 - 17) row represents the expenditure sum of all ages (0, 1, 2, 3,...17) in 2011 dollars. The figures represent estimated expenses on the younger child in a two-child family. Estimates are about the same for the older child, so to calculate expenses for two children, figures should be summed for the appropriate age categories. To estimate expenses for an only child, multiply the total expense for the appropriate age category by 1.25. To estimate expenses for each child in a family with three or more children, multiply the total expense for each appropriate age category by 0.78. For expenses on all children in a family, these totals should be summed.

The Northeastern region consists of Connecticut, Maine, Massachusetts, New Hampshire, New Jersey, New York, Pennsylvania, Rhode Island, and Vermont.

[a] Includes only families with child care and education expenses.

[b] Includes personal care items, entertainment, and reading materials.

Table 3. Estimated annual expenditures on a child by husband-wife families, urban West, 2011

Age of child	Total expense	Housing	Food	Transportation	Clothing	Health care	Child care and education[a]	Miscellaneous[b]
Before-tax income: Less than $58,890 (Average = $37,670)								
0 - 2	$9,870	$3,560	$1,210	$1,260	$680	$580	$2,030	$550
3 - 5	9,880	3,560	1,310	1,320	540	540	1,860	750
6 - 8	9,560	3,560	1,770	1,440	610	610	800	770
9 - 11	10,320	3,560	2,040	1,450	620	660	1,220	770
12 - 14	10,760	3,560	2,210	1,570	740	1,000	840	840
15 - 17	10,840	3,560	2,200	1,720	790	930	920	720
Total	**$183,690**	**$64,080**	**$32,220**	**$26,280**	**$11,940**	**$12,960**	**$23,010**	**$13,200**
Before-tax income: $58,890 to $101,960 (Average = $79,240)								
0 - 2	$13,250	$4,670	$1,440	$1,780	$800	$790	$2,750	$1,020
3 - 5	13,240	4,670	1,530	1,840	650	750	2,580	1,220
6 - 8	13,130	4,670	2,150	1,960	720	870	1,520	1,240
9 - 11	13,970	4,670	2,460	1,970	750	940	1,950	1,230

Age of child	Total expense	Housing	Food	Transportation	Clothing	Health care	Child care and education[a]	Miscellaneous[b]
12 - 14	14,650	4,670	2,640	2,090	890	1,320	1,740	1,300
15 - 17	15,160	4,670	2,630	2,240	970	1,240	2,230	1,180
Total	**$250,200**	**$84,060**	**$38,550**	**$35,640**	**$14,340**	**$17,730**	**$38,310**	**$21,570**
Before-tax income: More than $101,960 (Average = $178,450)								
0 - 2	$21,880	$8,450	$1,930	$2,640	$1,100	$920	$4,940	$1,900
3 - 5	21,830	8,450	2,020	2,700	920	870	4,770	2,100
6 - 8	21,800	8,450	2,660	2,830	1,010	1,020	3,710	2,120
9 - 11	22,680	8,450	3,020	2,830	1,050	1,080	4,130	2,120
12 - 14	24,060	8,450	3,230	2,950	1,240	1,520	4,480	2,190
15 - 17	25,830	8,450	3,220	3,100	1,350	1,430	6,210	2,070
Total	**$414,240**	**$152,100**	**$48,240**	**$51,150**	**$20,010**	**$20,520**	**$84,720**	**$37,500**

Estimates are based on 2005-06 Consumer Expenditure Survey data updated to 2011 dollars by using the regional Consumer Price Index. For each age category, the expense estimates represent average child-rearing expenditures for each age (e.g., the expense for the 3-5 age category, on average, applies to the 3-year-old, the 4-year-old, or the 5-year-old). The Total (0 - 17) row represents the expenditure sum of all ages (0, 1, 2, 3,...17) in 2011 dollars. The figures represent estimated expenses on the younger child in a two-child family. Estimates are about the same for the older child, so to calculate expenses for two children, figures should be summed for the appropriate age categories. To estimate expenses for an only child, multiply the total expense for the appropriate age category by 1.25. To estimate expenses for each child in a family with three or more children, multiply the total expense for each appropriate age category by 0.78. For expenses on all children in a family, these totals should be summed.

The Western region consists of Alaska, Arizona, California, Colorado, Hawaii, Idaho, Montana, Nevada, New Mexico, Oregon, Utah, Washington, and Wyoming.

[a] Includes only families with child care and education expenses.

[b] Includes personal care items, entertainment, and reading materials.

Table 4. Estimated annual expenditures on a child by husband-wife families, urban Midwest, 2011

Age of child	Total expense	Housing	Food	Transportation	Clothing	Health care	Child care and education[a]	Miscellaneous[b]
Before-tax income: Less than $59,250 (Average = $37,900)								
0 - 2	$8,950	$2,880	$1,100	$1,100	$620	$600	$2,170	$480
3 - 5	8,960	2,880	1,200	1,160	480	560	2,000	680
6 - 8	8,620	2,880	1,640	1,280	550	630	940	700
9 - 11	9,370	2,880	1,900	1,290	570	680	1,360	690
12 - 14	9,840	2,880	2,060	1,410	680	1,030	1,020	760
15 - 17	10,020	2,880	2,060	1,570	720	960	1,180	650
Total	**$167,280**	**$51,840**	**$29,880**	**$23,430**	**$10,860**	**$13,380**	**$26,010**	**$11,880**
Before-tax income: $59,250 to $102,590 (Average = $79,720)								
0 - 2	$12,140	$3,780	$1,340	$1,630	$750	$810	$2,890	$940
3 - 5	12,110	3,780	1,430	1,680	590	760	2,720	1,150
6 - 8	12,010	3,780	2,030	1,810	670	890	1,660	1,170
9 - 11	12,820	3,780	2,320	1,820	690	960	2,090	1,160
12 - 14	13,540	3,780	2,500	1,940	830	1,340	1,920	1,230
15 - 17	14,140	3,780	2,500	2,100	900	1,260	2,490	1,110
Total	**$230,280**	**$68,040**	**$36,360**	**$32,940**	**$13,290**	**$18,060**	**$41,310**	**$20,280**
Before-tax income: More than $102,590 (Average = $179,540)								
0 - 2	$20,070	$6,850	$1,830	$2,500	$1,030	$940	$5,080	$1,840
3 - 5	20,040	6,850	1,930	2,560	860	890	4,910	2,040
6 - 8	19,970	6,850	2,550	2,690	940	1,030	3,850	2,060
9 - 11	20,840	6,850	2,900	2,690	980	1,100	4,270	2,050
12 - 14	22,260	6,850	3,110	2,810	1,160	1,550	4,650	2,130

Age of child	Total expense	Housing	Food	Transportation	Clothing	Health care	Child care and education[a]	Miscellaneous[b]
15 - 17	24,130	6,850	3,100	2,970	1,270	1,460	6,470	2,010
Total	**$381,930**	**$123,300**	**$46,260**	**$48,660**	**$18,720**	**$20,910**	**$87,690**	**$36,390**

Estimates are based on 2005-06 Consumer Expenditure Survey data updated to 2012 dollars by using the regional Consumer Price Index. For each age category, the expense estimates represent average child-rearing expenditures for each age (e.g., the expense for the 3-5 age category, on average, applies to the 3-year-old, the 4-year-old, or the 5-year-old). The Total (0 - 17) row represents the expenditure sum of all ages (0, 1, 2, 3, ...17) in 2012 dollars. The figures represent estimated expenses on the younger child in a two-child family. Estimates are about the same for the older child, so to calculate expenses for two children, figures should be summed for the appropriate age categories. To estimate expenses for an only child, multiply the total expense for the appropriate age category by 1.25. To estimate expenses for each child in a family with three or more children, multiply the total expense for each appropriate age category by 0.78. For expenses on all children in a family, these totals should be summed.

The Midwestern region consists of Illinois, Indiana, Iowa, Kansas, Michigan, Minnesota, Missouri, Nebraska, North Dakota, Ohio, South Dakota, and Wisconsin.

[a] Includes only families with child care and education expenses.

[b] Includes personal care items, entertainment, and reading materials.

Table 5. Estimated annual expenditures on a child by husband-wife families, urban South, 2011

Age of child	Total expense	Housing	Food	Transportation	Clothing	Health care	Child care and education[a]	Miscellaneous[b]
Before-tax income: Less than $59,790 (Average = $38,240)								
0 - 2	$8,470	$2,700	$1,160	$1,120	$620	$590	$1,980	$300
3 - 5	8,490	2,700	1,260	1,180	490	550	1,810	500
6 - 8	8,170	2,700	1,720	1,310	550	620	750	520
9 - 11	8,930	2,700	1,980	1,310	570	670	1,180	520

Table 5. (Continued)

Age of child	Total expense	Housing	Food	Transportation	Clothing	Health care	Child care and education[a]	Miscellaneous[b]
12 - 14	9,350	2,700	2,150	1,440	680	1,010	780	590
15 - 17	9,390	2,700	2,140	1,590	720	940	830	470
Total	**$158,400**	**$48,600**	**$31,230**	**$23,850**	**$10,890**	**$13,140**	**$21,990**	**$8,700**
Before-tax income: $59,790 to $103,530 (Average = $80,450)								
0 - 2	$11,620	$3,550	$1,400	$1,660	$740	$800	$2,700	$770
3 - 5	11,590	3,550	1,490	1,710	590	750	2,530	970
6 - 8	11,520	3,550	2,110	1,840	670	880	1,480	990
9 - 11	12,320	3,550	2,410	1,850	690	940	1,900	980
12 - 14	13,010	3,550	2,590	1,970	830	1,330	1,680	1,060
15 - 17	13,510	3,550	2,590	2,130	900	1,250	2,150	940
Total	**$220,710**	**$63,900**	**$37,770**	**$33,480**	**$13,260**	**$17,850**	**$37,320**	**$17,130**
Before-tax income: More than $103,530 (Average = $181,180)								
0 - 2	$19,350	$6,420	$1,900	$2,530	$1,020	$930	$4,890	$1,660
3 - 5	19,310	6,420	1,990	2,590	850	880	4,720	1,860
6 - 8	19,270	6,420	2,630	2,720	940	1,020	3,660	1,880
9 - 11	20,140	6,420	2,980	2,720	970	1,090	4,090	1,870
12 - 14	21,500	6,420	3,190	2,850	1,150	1,530	4,420	1,940
15 - 17	23,250	6,420	3,190	3,000	1,260	1,440	6,120	1,820
Total	**$368,460**	**$115,560**	**$47,640**	**$49,230**	**$18,570**	**$20,670**	**$83,700**	**$33,090**

Estimates are based on 2005-06 Consumer Expenditure Survey data updated to 2011 dollars by using the regional Consumer Price Index. For each age category, the expense estimates represent average child-rearing expenditures for each age (e.g., the expense for the 3-5 age category, on average, applies to the 3-year-old, the 4-year-old, or the 5-year-old). The Total (0 - 17) row represents the expenditure sum of all ages (0, 1, 2, 3,...17) in 2011 dollars. The figures represent estimated expenses on the younger child in a two-child family. Estimates are about the same for the older child, so to calculate expenses for two children, figures should be summed for the appropriate age categories. To estimate expenses for an only child, multiply the total expense for the appropriate age category by 1.25. To estimate expenses for each child in a family with three or more children, multiply the total expense for each appropriate age category by 0.78. For expenses on all children in a family, these totals should be summed.

The Southern region consists of Alabama, Arkansas, Delaware, District of Columbia, Florida, Georgia, Kentucky, Louisiana, Maryland, Mississippi, North Carolina, Oklahoma, South Carolina, Tennessee, Texas, Virginia, and West Virginia.

[a] Includes only families with child care and education expenses.

[b] Includes personal care items, entertainment, and reading materials.

Table 6. Estimated annual expenditures on a child by husband-wife families, rural areas, 2011

Age of child	Total expense	Housing	Food	Transportation	Clothing	Health care	Child care and education[a]	Miscellaneous[b]
Before-tax income: Less than $60,020 (Average = $38,390)								
0 - 2	$7,590	$1,840	$1,020	$1,270	$620	$620	$1,840	$380
3 - 5	7,190	1,840	1,120	1,330	490	590	1,230	590
6 - 8	7,320	1,840	1,540	1,460	550	650	670	610
9 - 11	7,600	1,840	1,800	1,460	560	700	640	600
12 - 14	8,210	1,840	1,950	1,590	670	1,070	420	670
15 - 17	8,400	1,840	1,950	1,740	700	1,000	620	550
Total	**$138,930**	**$33,120**	**$28,140**	**$26,550**	**$10,770**	**$13,890**	**$16,260**	**$10,200**
Before-tax income: $60,020 to $103,920 (Average = $80,760)								
0 - 2	$9,910	$2,410	$1,260	$1,800	$730	$840	$2,020	$850
3 – 5	9,490	2,410	1,360	1,860	590	800	1,410	1,060

Table 6. (Continued)

Age of child	Total expense	Housing	Food	Transportation	Clothing	Health care	Child care and education[a]	Miscellaneous[b]
6 - 8	9,850	2,410	1,930	1,990	660	930	850	1,080
9 - 11	10,190	2,410	2,220	1,990	680	990	830	1,070
12 - 14	10,920	2,410	2,400	2,120	810	1,390	650	1,140
15 - 17	11,210	2,410	2,390	2,270	870	1,310	940	1,020
Total	**$184,710**	**$43,380**	**$34,680**	**$36,090**	**$13,020**	**$18,780**	**$20,100**	**$18,660**
Before-tax income: More than $103,920 (Average = $181,870)								
0 - 2	$15,680	$4,370	$1,760	$2,680	$1,010	$970	$3,140	$1,750
3 - 5	15,220	4,370	1,860	2,740	850	930	2,520	1,950
6 - 8	15,650	4,370	2,470	2,870	930	1,070	1,970	1,970
9 - 11	16,060	4,370	2,810	2,870	960	1,140	1,940	1,970
12 - 14	17,200	4,370	3,010	3,000	1,130	1,600	2,050	2,040
15 - 17	18,160	4,370	3,000	3,150	1,230	1,510	2,980	1,920
Total	**$293,910**	**$78,660**	**$44,730**	**$51,930**	**$18,330**	**$21,660**	**$43,800**	**$34,800**

Estimates are based on 2005-06 Consumer Expenditure Survey data updated to 2011 dollars by using the population size Consumer Price Index. For each age category, the expense estimates represent average child-rearing expenditures for each age (e.g., the expense for the 3-5 age category, on average, applies to the 3-year-old, the 4-year-old, or the 5-year-old). The Total (0 - 17) row represents the expenditure sum of all ages (0, 1, 2, 3,...17) in 2011 dollars. The figures represent estimated expenses on the younger child in a two-child family. Estimates are about the same for the older child, so to calculate expenses for two children, figures should be summed for the appropriate age categories. To estimate expenses for an only child, multiply the total expense for the appropriate age category by 1.25. To estimate expenses for each child in a family with three or more children, multiply the total expense for each appropriate age category by 0.78.

For expenses on all children in a family, these totals should be summed.

Rural areas are places of fewer than 2,500 people outside a Metropolitan Statistical Area.

[a] Includes only families with child care and education expenses.

[b] Includes personal care items, entertainment, and reading materials.

Table 7. Estimated annual expenditures on a child by single-parent families, overall United States, 2011

Age of child	Total expense	Housing	Food	Transportation	Clothing	Health care	Child care and education[a]	Miscellaneous[b]
Before-tax income: Less than $59,410 (Average = $26,350)								
0 - 2	$7,760	$2,840	$1,400	$680	$410	$520	$1,400	$510
3 - 5	8,610	2,840	1,370	920	330	600	1,940	610
6 - 8	8,450	2,840	1,830	1,030	340	670	960	780
9 - 11	9,030	2,840	2,010	1,060	400	620	1,360	740
12 - 14	9,440	2,840	2,150	1,130	420	940	1,120	840
15 - 17	9,180	2,840	2,270	1,130	460	930	880	670
Total	**$157,410**	**$51,120**	**$33,090**	**$17,850**	**$7,080**	**$12,840**	**$22,980**	**$12,450**
Before-tax income: $59,410 or more (Average = $107,820)								
0 - 2	$16,770	$5,880	$2,080	$1,920	$590	$980	$3,670	$1,650
3 - 5	17,660	5,880	2,070	2,160	500	1,090	4,210	1,750
6 - 8	17,810	5,880	2,680	2,260	530	1,180	3,350	1,930
9 - 11	18,660	5,880	3,000	2,300	610	1,110	3,880	1,880
12 - 14	19,670	5,880	3,080	2,370	650	1,560	4,150	1,980
15 - 17	20,570	5,880	3,220	2,370	730	1,550	5,010	1,810
Total	**$333,420**	**$105,840**	**$48,390**	**$40,140**	**$10,830**	**$22,410**	**$72,810**	**$33,000**

Estimates are based on 2005-06 Consumer Expenditure Survey data updated to 2011 dollars by using the Consumer Price Index. For each age category, the expense estimates represent average child-rearing expenditures for each age (e.g., the expense for the 3-5 age category, on average, applies to the 3-year-old, the 4-year-old, or the 5-year-old). The Total (0 - 17) row represents the expenditure sum of all ages (0, 1, 2, 3, ...17) in 2011 dollars. The figures represent estimated expenses on the younger child in a single-parent, two-child family. For estimated expenses on the older child, multiply the total expense for the appropriate age category by 0.97. To estimate expenses for two children, the expenses on the younger child and older child after adjusting the expense on the older child downward should be summed for the appropriate age categories. To estimate expenses for an only child, multiply the total expense for the appropriate age category by 1.29. To estimate expenses for each child in a family with three or more children, multiply the total expense for each appropriate age category by 0.77 after adjusting the expenses on the older children downward. For expenses on all children in a family, these totals should be summed.

[a] Includes only families with child care and education expenses.

[b] Includes personal care items, entertainment, and reading materials.

Selected Results

- Child-rearing expenses vary considerably by household income level. For a child in a two- child, husband-wife family, annual expenses ranged from $8,760 to $9,970, on average, (depending on age of the child) for households with before-tax income less than $59,410, from $12,290 to $14,320 for households with before-tax income between $59,410 and $102,870, and from $20,420 to $24,510 for households with before-tax income more than $102,870.
- As a proportion of total child-rearing expenses, housing accounted for the largest share across income groups, comprising 30 to 32 percent of total expenses on a child in a two-child, husband-wife family. For families in the middle-income group, child care/education (for those with the expense) and food were the next largest average expenditures on a child, accounting for 18 and 16 percent of child-rearing expenses, respectively.
- Annual expenditures on children generally increased with age of the child. This fact was the same for both husband-wife and single-parent families.
- Overall annual child-rearing expenses were highest for husband-wife families in the urban Northeast, followed by families in the urban West and urban Midwest; families in the urban South and rural areas had the lowest child-rearing expenses.
- Compared with expenditures on each child in a two-child, husband-wife family, expenditures by husband-wife households with one child average 25 percent more on the single child and expenditures by households with three or more children average 22 percent less on each child.
- Child-rearing expense patterns of single-parent households with a before-tax income less than $59,410 were 7 percent lower than those of husband-wife households in the same income group. Most single-parent households were in this income group (compared with about one-third of husband-wife families).

Other Expenditures on Children

Expenditures for major budgetary components estimated in this study consisted of direct parental expenses made on children through age 17. These expenditures exclude college costs and other parental expenses on children after age 17. In addition, expenditures on children made by people outside the household and by the government are not included. Indirect costs involved in child rearing by parents (time costs and foregone earnings and career opportunities) are also not included in the estimates.

EXPENDITURES ON CHILDREN BY FAMILIES, 2011

The U.S. Department of Agriculture (USDA) has provided estimates of expenditures on children from birth through age 17 since 1960. These estimates may be used in developing State child support guidelines and foster care payments, as well as in family education programs. This report presents 2011 estimated child-rearing expenses by husband-wife and single-parent families. The figures for 2011 are shown in tables 1-7 at the end of this report. The 2011 USDA estimates are not directly comparable to previous estimates (U.S. Department of Agriculture, 1981; Lino, 2008) because of changes in methods.

For husband-wife families, child-rearing expenses are for three income groups and for single- parent families, two income groups. To adjust partially for price differentials and varying patterns of expenditures, USDA also provides estimates for husband-wife families in various regions, as well as the United States overall. For single-parent families, estimates are provided only for the United States overall because of limitations in sample size. For all families, expenditures on children are estimated for the major budgetary components: Housing, food, transportation, clothing, health care, child care and education, and miscellaneous goods and services (entertainment, personal care items, etc.).

This report presents the USDA methodology for deriving expenditures on children and the results. First, data used in determining child-rearing expenditures will be described. These data contain overall household expenditures for some budgetary components and child-specific expenditures for other components. Overall household expenditures must be allocated among family members to determine expenses on children. Second, the allocation methods used by USDA will be explained, along with general estimation techniques. Third, an overview of the results will be given. Fourth, how the USDA estimates on child-rearing expenses compare with the results of alternative methodologies on estimating child-rearing expenses will be discussed. The report ends with an explanation of how future child-rearing expenses may be determined and a discussion on other expenses on children not included in this report.

Estimating and Allocating Expenditures on Children

Data Used

Since 1960, the first year USDA produced child-rearing expense estimates, the Consumer Expenditure Survey (CE) has been used as the basis for the estimates. The CE is also used in alternative methodologies on estimating child-rearing expenses. CE data are the most comprehensive source of information on household expenditures available at the national level, containing expenditure data for housing, food, transportation, clothing, health care, child care and education, and miscellaneous goods and services (the box below describes the specific items in each expenditure component).

CATEGORIES OF HOUSEHOLD EXPENDITURES

Housing expenses consist of shelter (mortgage payments, property taxes, or rent; maintenance and repairs; and insurance), utilities (gas, electricity, fuel, cell/telephone, and water), and house furnishings and equipment (furniture, floor coverings, major appliances, and small appliances). Mortgage payments included principal and interest payments. Overall, principal payments constituted 15 percent of overall housing expenses.

Food expenses consist of food and nonalcoholic beverages purchased at grocery, convenience, and specialty stores, including purchases with Food Stamp Program (now the Supplemental Nutrition Assistance Program) benefits; dining at restaurants; and household expenditures on school meals.

Transportation expenses consist of the monthly payments on vehicle loans, downpayments, gasoline and motor oil, maintenance and repairs, insurance, and public transportation (including airline fares).

Clothing expenses consist of children's apparel such as diapers, shirts, pants, dresses, and suits; footwear; and clothing services such as dry cleaning, alterations, and repair.

Health care expenses consist of medical and dental services not covered by insurance, prescription drugs and medical supplies not covered by insurance, and health insurance premiums not paid by an employer or other organization. Medical services include those related to physical and mental health.

Child care and education expenses consist of day care tuition and supplies; baby-sitting; and elementary and high school tuition, books, fees, and supplies. Books, fees, and supplies may be for private or public schools.

Miscellaneous expenses consist of personal care items (haircuts, toothbrushes, etc.), entertainment (portable media players, sports equipment, televisions, computers, etc.), and reading materials (nonschool books, magazines, etc.).

USDA's latest estimates are based on data from the 2005-06 CE—Interview Survey component. Administered by the U.S. Census Bureau, U.S. Department of Commerce, under contract with the Bureau of Labor Statistics (BLS), U.S. Department of Labor, the CE collects information on characteristics, income, and expenditures of consumer units. For this study, the terms households and families are used for consumer units. During most of 2005-06, about 7,000 to 7,800 households were interviewed each quarter, bringing the total number of interviews in each year's survey to over 28,000. Due to the rotating sample design of the Interview Survey, each sample household could be interviewed up to four consecutive quarters over the 2-year period. Households report expenditures for the 3 months prior to the interview month. Since the households interviewed each quarter are deemed an independent sample by BLS, the 3-month expenditures they report may be annualized (U.S. Department of Labor, 2007) for analytical purposes.

Child-rearing expenses of 11,800 husband-wife and 3,350 single-parent families where the parents were ages 20 to 60 were examined. These households had at least one child of their own, age 17 or under, in the household, and there were no other related or unrelated people present in the household except their own children. Most single-parent families (85 percent) were headed by a woman. BLS methods were used to weight all data to reflect the U.S. population of interest.

Although based on 2005-06 data, the expense estimates were updated to 2011 dollars by using the Consumer Price Index (CPI). Expenditure and income data for 2005 were first converted to 2006 dollars, analysis was undertaken, and then the resulting estimations were updated to 2011 dollars. Income levels of households were updated to 2011 dollars by using the all-items category of the CPI, and expenditures were updated by using the CPI for the corresponding budgetary component (i.e., the CPIs for housing, food, etc.). Regional CPIs were used to update the regional estimates to 2011 dollars.

Although the CE provides the best available data for estimating spending on children, it has its limitations. The CE contains overall household expenditure data for some budgetary components (housing, food, transportation, health care, and miscellaneous goods and services) and child-specific expenditure data for other components (children's clothing, child care, and education). Thus, to estimate child-rearing expenses, these household-level expenditures must be allocated among family members. The next sections describe the methodology used by USDA to allocate these household expenditures. Two different models were used, one to determine food, transportation, health care, clothing, child care and education, and miscellaneous expenses on children, and the other to determine housing expenses on children.

Determining Food, Transportation, Health Care, Clothing, Child Care and Education, and Miscellaneous Expenses on Children

For these budgetary components, multivariate analyses were used to estimate household and child-specific expenditures. These analyses controlled for income level, family size, and age of the younger child so that estimates could be made for families with these varying characteristics. The estimation model, conducted separately for husband-wife and single- parent households, for the overall United States was:

$$E_i = f(Y, HS, CA) \quad (1)$$

where:

E_i = household expenditures on a particular budgetary component (food, transportation, health care, children's clothing, child care and education, and miscellaneous goods and services)

Y = household before-tax income (divided into three groups for husband-wife families: < \$59,410, \$59,410 to \$102,870, and > \$102,870 in 2011 dollars, and two groups for single-parent families: <\$59,410 and \$59,410 or more in 2011 dollars)

HS = number of children in the household (divided into three groups: 1 child, 2 children, and 3 or more children)

CA = age of the younger child (divided into six age groups: 0-2, 3-5, 6-8, 9-11, 12-14, and 15-17)

For the regional estimates of expenditures on children in husband-wife households, the model was:

$$E_i = f(Y, HS, CA, RG) \tag{2}$$

where E_i through CA are the same as before and

RG = region (divided into five regions: urban Northeast, urban South, urban Midwest, urban West, and rural areas)

Ordinary Least Squares analysis was used to estimate expenditures on food, transportation, child care and education, and miscellaneous goods and services. Tobit analysis was used to estimate expenditures on health care and children's clothing because although most households had an expenditure on these budgetary components, over 10 percent reported zero expenses. Because of these zero expenditures, tobit analysis yields statistically better (unbiased) estimates than does Ordinary Least Squares analysis. The procedure outlined by McDonald and Moffitt (1980) was used to transform the estimates resulting from the tobit analysis into dollars. The coefficients of the estimates were used to calculate the expenditures for the budgetary components for each income group, age of the younger child, and region (for husband-wife families) for a two-child family. Households with two children were selected as the standard because two children was the average for husband-wife and single-parent families in 2005-06 based on CE data. Age of the older child was not controlled for because the focus was on the younger child and by doing so, results would only be applicable to families with an older child in a certain age category. It was therefore assumed the distribution of age ranges of the older child was similar across families. Also, additional analysis focused on the older child (see "Adjustments for Older Children and Household Size" section). Typically, the older child was 3 to 4 years older then the younger child and under age 18.

The three income groups of husband-wife households (before-tax income under $59,410, between $59,410 and $102,870, and over $102,870 in 2011 dollars) were determined by dividing the sample of husband-wife families for the overall United States into equal thirds. Income intervals were used to be consistent with previous USDA studies. These three income groups will be referred to as the lower (although most families in this group are above the poverty threshold), middle, and higher income groups. Income groups of single-parent households (before-tax income under $59,410 and $59,410 and over in 2011 dollars) were selected to correspond with the income groups used for husband-wife households for comparison purposes, that is, to see how child-rearing expenditures differed between husband-wife and single-parent households in the same income group. This income includes child-support payments. The two higher income groups used with husband-wife families were combined in the case of single-parent families because only 15 percent of these households had a before-tax income of $59,410 and over.

Estimates were made for six age categories of younger children (0-2, 3-5, 6-8, 9-11, 12-14, and 15-17 years) because spending on children differs by age of the child. These age categories approximate the different stages of childhood and have historically been used. The focus was on the younger child in a household because the older child was sometimes over age 17. If the older child had been selected as the household member of interest, expenditures may be different. Also, if households with one or three or more children had been selected, per-child expenditures would reflect the differences in family size. As the number of children in a family increases, the allocation of resources among children changes. To adjust expenditures for the older child and number of children, see discussion beginning on page 15.

For husband-wife families, estimates are provided for the urban Northeast, urban South, urban Midwest, urban West, and rural areas overall, as well as for the overall United States. Urban areas are defined as Metropolitan Statistical Areas (MSAs) and other places of 2,500 or more people outside an MSA; rural areas are places of fewer than 2,500 people outside an MSA. Sample sizes were not sufficient to conduct regional analysis for single-parent families.

Once the expenditures on the budgetary components were estimated, they were allocated to children. The allocation methods varied by budgetary component and are described below.

Clothing

The CE collects data on how much families are spending on children's shoes, pants, dresses, and so on. Hence, estimated expenditures for clothing may be readily assigned to children. It was assumed these expenses were equally allocated to each child in the two-child household when both children were less than age 18. CE data on children's clothing expenditures were for children age 15 and under. For the estimates, it was assumed the clothing expenditures of a 16- or 17-year-old were similar to those of a 15-year-old; thus, these older teenagers were assigned the expenditures of a 15-year-old. Also, expenditures for clothing services (dry cleaning, alterations, etc.), which account for a smaller proportion of total clothing expenses, were esti- mated for the overall household and allocated on a per capita basis among household members.

Child Care and Education

Child care and education was the only budgetary component for which about half of all households reported no expenditure. Expenditure on this budgetary component rose with household income level: For husband-wife families, 31 percent in the lower income group had this expenditure, compared with 45 and 56 percent in the middle and higher income groups; for single-parent families, the percentages were 34 and 44 percent for the lower and higher income groups. Previous USDA estimates of child care/education expenses on a child consisted of households with the expense as well as households without the expense. However, to be more applicable to families, this update included only those families with the expense. For families without child care/education expenses, this budgetary component would amount to zero; therefore, total expenditures on a child should be adjusted to account for this.

As with clothing, estimated expenditures for child care/education in the CE were only for the children in the household so may be readily assigned to them. It was assumed these expenses were equally allocated to each child in the two-child household when both children were less than age 18. For preschool children, most of this budgetary-component expenditure is for child care, whereas for older children, most of this expenditure is for education (a major reason the two components are combined; otherwise, many age categories would have a negligible expense either for one or the other). The child care figures include families with part-time child care on a regular or irregular basis; therefore, they appear low when compared with those with full-time care. For more detailed analysis of average weekly child care expenses for families with the expense, see U.S. Census Bureau (2011). It should be noted that by only including households with child care/education expenses, the total expenses on a child as a result of summing the budgetary components may be overestimated because those with child care/education expenses may have to draw from other child-rearing budgetary components (e.g., housing, transportation, miscellaneous) to pay for it.

Food

Although the CE did not collect expenditures on food by family member, data from the 2008 USDA food plans (U.S. Department of Agriculture, 2008) are used to calculate the shares of total household food expenses spent on children. These shares were used to apportion house- hold food expenses by age of the household member, household size, and income. The USDA food plans are based on household food use and individual intake, as well as food expenditure data. The food plans also reflect the cost of a nutritious diet, which accounts for food costs, nutritional needs, and consumption behavior. These food budget shares, as derived from the USDA food plans, were applied to estimated household food expenditures to determine food expenses on children. The food budget shares ranged between 17 to 25 percent for a child in a two-child, husband-wife family and 25 to 34 percent for a child in a two-child, single-parent family (these shares being higher for a three-person household). Food budget shares generally increased with the age of the child and did not vary much by household income level.

Health Care

Like food, expenditures on health care by family members were not collected by the CE. Data from other sources—in this case, the U.S. Department of Health and Human Services' 2005 Medical Expenditure Panel Survey—show the share of household out-of-pocket health care expenses spent on children. These shares were used to apportion family health care expenses by age of the household member, household size, and income. The Medical Expenditure Panel Survey is a nationally representative longitudinal survey that collects detailed information on health care utilization and expenditures, health insurance, and health status, as well as a wide variety of social, demographic, and economic characteristics for the civilian noninstitutionalized population. (See Bernard, 2007, for more information about this survey, as well as for out-of-pocket expenditures on health care.)

These health care budget shares, as derived from the survey, were applied to estimated house- hold health care expenditures to determine health care expenses on children. The health care budget shares ranged between 16 to 25 percent for a child in a two-child, husband-wife family and 24 to 33 percent for a child in a two-child, single-parent family (these shares again being higher for a three-person household). Health care budget shares generally increased with the age of the child and did not vary much by household income level. As an example of how health care expenditures were calculated on a 6- to 8-year-old, who is the younger child in a husband-wife, two-child household in the middle-income group, overall household health care expenditures were estimated from the multivariate analysis to be $5,222 in 2011 dollars for this family type. Based on the Medical Expenditure Panel Survey, the health care budget share for this 6- to 8-year-old was figured to be 18 percent. Thus, health care expenditures on the 6- to 8-year-old were estimated to be $940 (=$5,222 X 0.18).

Transportation

Transportation expenses related only to family-related activities were examined when determining child-rearing transportation expenses. These activities accounted for 59 percent of total transportation, according to a U.S. Department of Transportation study (Hu & Reuscher, 2004). Other transportation expenses, mainly those due to employment, as well as some household maintenance, are not related directly to expenses on children, so these types of transportation expenses were excluded.

Unlike data for food and health care, no other data show the share of transportation expenses associated with child rearing. Hence, to allocate these expenses, the per capita method was used to determine family-related transportation expenses on a child by allocating in equal proportions the expenses among household members. One of the first studies on child-rearing expenses also used the per capita approach to allocate transportation expenses among family members (Dublin & Lotka, 1946). The per capita method for allocating transportation does not account for some families driving larger vehicles because of children, likely leading to underestimates of transportation expenses on children. Although the per capita method has its limitations, these were judged less severe than those of alternative approaches (see the "Alternative Estimates of Expenditures on Children" section of this report). For a child in a two-child, husband-wife family, the per capita method (factoring in only family-related travel) resulted in approximately 15 percent of total transportation expenses being allocated to the child; for a child in a two-child, single-parent family, 20 percent.

Miscellaneous Expenses

As with expenditures on transportation, no other data show the share of miscellaneous expenses (personal care items, such as haircuts, toothbrushes, etc.; entertainment, such as portable media players, sports equipment, computers, etc.; and reading materials, such as nonschool books, magazines, etc.) attributed to child rearing. Therefore, the per capita method was used to apportion miscellaneous expenses among family members. For many of the goods and services in this budgetary component, such as fees and admissions, videos, and personal care items, the per capita method is reasonable because such goods and services are likely to be equally shared by family members.

Determining Housing Expenses on Children

One method to estimate housing expenses on a child is to track families over time and see how their housing expenses change exclusively as a result of children being added to the household. One would expect families to increase their housing expenditures as they move to larger residences to accommodate children. Child-related housing costs could therefore be calculated by utilizing these additional costs. However, CE data have annual family housing expenses. So, to determine child-rearing housing expenses, one must use this information.

Based on the rationale that over time the presence of a child in a home does not affect the number of kitchens or living rooms, but does affect the number of bedrooms (analysis of CE data confirmed this), the average cost of an additional bedroom approach was used to estimate housing expenses on a child in husband-wife and single-parent households. Previously, a per capita approach was used by USDA to estimate children's housing expenses, where housing expenses were assigned to household members in equal proportions. Because more data on housing characteristics have been made available in the CE survey over time, this average cost of an additional bedroom approach was developed. Specifically, this approach calculates child-rearing housing expenses as the extra housing costs associated with an additional bedroom in a home for families with children and in each income interval. Multivariate analysis was used to determine the average additional costs by regressing housing expenditures on the number of bedrooms in a home controlling for income level. The analysis was conducted separately for husband-wife and single-parent families. Housing expenses were adjusted to account for regional variation in the case of husband-wife families.

Because most families with children resided in a three- or four-bedroom home, housing expenses on a child were calculated as the average additional cost of one (but not both) of these bedrooms. It was assumed that children in a two-child family do not share a bedroom. With this method, housing expenses on a child include the costs of utilities and furniture associated with the additional bedroom. These expenses also do not vary by age of the child because costs due to the bedroom would not be expected to differ much by age.

The average cost of an additional bedroom approach is a conservative estimate of housing expenses on children because it does not account fully for the fact that some families pay more for housing to live in a community with good schools or other amenities for children. Part of this expense is captured in the cost of the additional bedroom, but parents may be spending more on their own housing to live in certain communities than they would without children. In addition, it is a conservative estimate because it does not account fully for parents' purchasing of a home with a larger yard, a playroom, or child-specific furnishings in other rooms of the home because of children in the household; however, data on these housing characteristics are limited.

A variation of the average cost of an additional bedroom approach that could account for these factors (better schools, larger yards, etc.) would be to compare the extra housing expenses due to an additional bedroom of couples with children with the expenses of couples without children. Initial estimates based on this variation resulted in slightly higher housing expenses on a child than reported here. This approach was ultimately not used because of difficulties in establishing a comparison group of childless families not composed of "empty nest" households at various income levels.

In addition, it is likely that younger couples without children buy larger houses in anticipation of having children. Comparing the expenditures of these couples with those of similar couples with children could lead to underestimates of housing expenditures on children because couples without children have incorporated possible future children in their housing expenditures. For single-parent households, selection of a comparison group is difficult. Single individuals (with no children) would include many people spending more on housing because they do not have child-rearing obligations. Using the housing expense difference between these people and single-parent families could lead to severe underestimates of housing expenditures on children in single-parent families.

For more information on how the USDA child-rearing housing expense estimates compare to alternative methodologies, including per capita and marginal cost approaches, and how they may be adjusted to reflect these alternative methodologies, see Lino and Carlson (2010).

Results

Complete estimates of child-rearing expenditures by husband-wife and single-parent families are contained in tables 1-7 at the end of this report. The following sections discuss major findings regarding these child-rearing expenditures.

Husband-Wife Families

Child-Rearing Expenses and Household Income Are Positively Related

In 2011, estimated annual average expenses on the younger child in two-child, husband-wife families increased as income level rose (figure 1). Depending on age of the child, annual expenses ranged from $8,760 to $9,970 for families with a before-tax income less than $59,410, from $12,290 to $14,320 for families with a before-tax income between $59,410 and $102,870, and from $20,420 to $24,510 for families with a before-tax income more than $102,870.

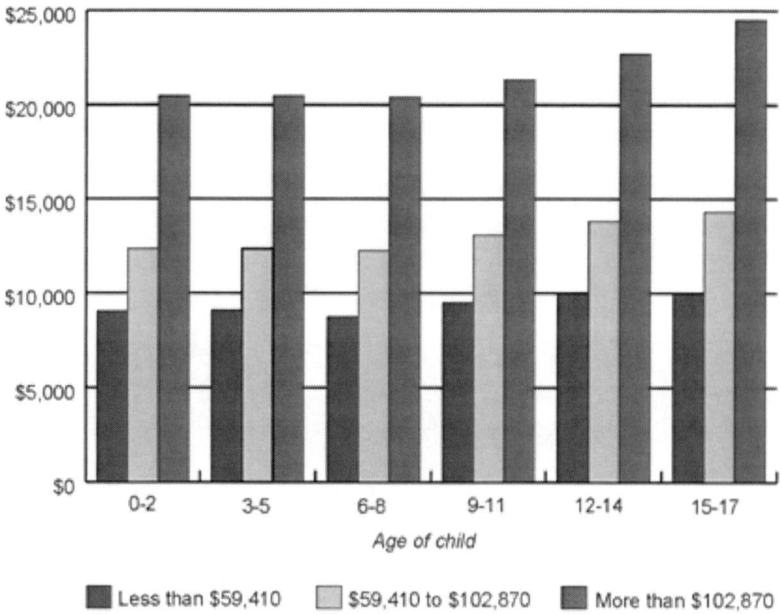

[1] U.S. average for the younger child in husband-wife families with two children.

Figure 1. Family expenditures on a child, by income level and age of child,[1] 2011.

On average, households in the lowest income group spent 25 percent of their before-tax income on a child; those in the middle-income group, 16 percent; and those in the highest group, 12 percent. The range among these percentages would be narrower if after-tax income were considered.

The amount spent on a child by families in the highest income group, on average, was more than twice the amount spent by families in the lowest income group. This amount varied by budgetary component. In general, expenses on a child for goods and services considered to be necessities (e.g., food and clothing) did not vary as much as those considered to be discretionary (e.g., miscellaneous expenses) among households in the three income groups.

Housing Is the Largest Expense on a Child

Housing accounted for the largest share of total child-rearing expenses. Figure 2 demonstrates this for the younger child in husband-wife, middle-income families with two children. Based on expenses incurred among all age groups, housing accounted for 32 percent of child-rearing expenses for a child in the lowest income group, 30 percent in the middle-income group, and 32 percent in the highest income group.

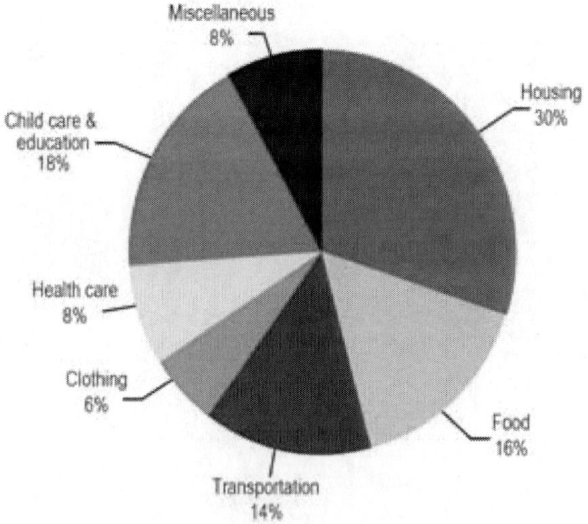

[1] U.S. average for the younger child in middle-income, husband-wife families with two children. Child care and education expenses only for families with expense.

Figure 2. Expenditure shares on a child from birth through age 17 as a percentage of total child-rearing expenditures,[1] 2011.

As previously discussed, child care and education was the only budgetary component for which many households had a zero expenditure and the others had a positive expenditure. The USDA estimates include only families with expenditures on this budgetary component. For the middle and highest income groups (for households with the expense), child care and education was the second largest expenditure on a child, accounting for 18 and 23 percent of child-rearing expenses, respectively. For the lowest income group, child care and education accounted for 14 percent of total child-rearing expenses (again, for households with the expense). It should be noted for lower income families, child care may be provided by relatives or friends at no cost due to affordability issues.

Food was the second largest expense on a child for families in the lowest income group, accounting for 18 percent of total expenditures. Food was the third largest expense on a child for families in the middle income group, accounting for 16 percent of total expenditures. Transportation made up 13 to 15 percent of total child-rearing expenses over the income groups.

Across the three income groups, miscellaneous goods and services accounted for 6 to 9 percent of child-rearing expenses; clothing (excluding gifts or hand-me-downs), 5 to 7 percent; and health care, 6 to 8 percent. Expenditures for health care consist of out-of-pocket expenses only (including insurance premiums not paid by an employer or other organizations) and not that portion covered by health insurance. Annual expenditures on clothing for teens, as based on the CE data, are similar to the findings of another survey of annual spending on teen apparel (PiperJaffray, 2010).

Expenses Increase as a Child Ages

Expenditures on a child in husband-wife families were generally lower in the younger age categories and higher in the older age categories. Figure 3 depicts this for families in the middle-income group. This relationship held across income groups. For all three income groups, food, transportation, clothing, and health care expenses on a child generally increased as the child grew older. As children age, they have greater nutritional needs so consume more food. Transportation expenses were highest for a child age 15 to 17, when he or she would start driving. Child care and education expenses were generally highest for a child under age 6. Most of this expense may be attributed to child care at this age.

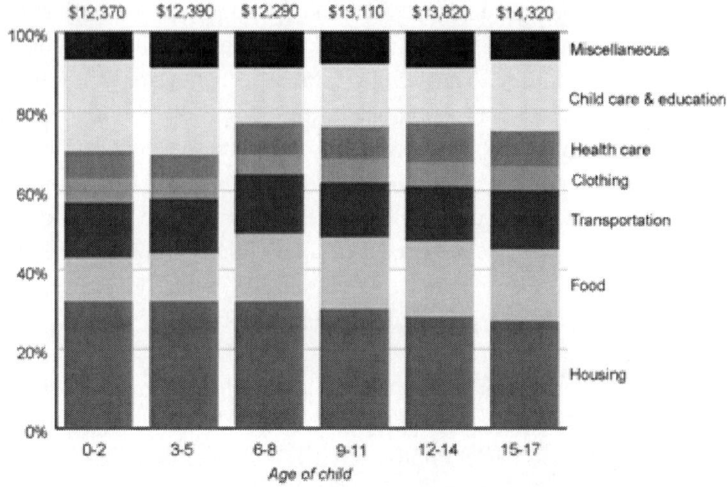

[1] U.S. average for the younger child in middle-income, husband-wife families with two children. Child care and education expenses only for families with expense.

Figure 3. Total expenses and expenditure shares on a child (as a percentage of total child-rearing expenditures), by age of child,1 2011.

Child-Rearing Expenses Are Highest in the Urban Northeast

Child-rearing expenses in the regions of the country reflect patterns observed in the overall United States for husband-wife families: In each region, expenses on a child increased with household income level and typically with age of the child. Figure 4 shows total child-rearing expenses by region and age of a child for the younger child in middle-income, two-child families. Overall, child-rearing expenses were highest in the urban Northeast, followed by the urban West and urban Midwest. Child-rearing expenses were lowest in the urban South and rural areas. Much of the regional difference in expenses on a child was related to housing costs and child care and education expenses. Total housing expenses on a child were highest in the urban Northeast and urban West and lowest in rural areas. Child care and education expenses were highest for families in the urban Northeast. Child-rearing transportation expenses were highest for families in the urban West and rural areas. This likely reflects the longer traveling distances in these areas.

Single-Parent Families

Expenses on a child in single-parent families generally followed the same pattern as expenses on a child in husband-wife families: Expenses increased as household income level rose; housing, food, and child care/education (for those with the expense) accounted for the largest budgetary shares; and more was spent as children aged. An interesting question is, "How do child-rearing expenses of single-parent families compare with those of husband-wife families?"

Figure 5 presents a comparison of estimated expenditures on a younger child in a two-child, husband-wife and single-parent household with a before-tax income less than $59,410; as previously discussed, 85 percent of single-parent families and 33 percent of husband-wife families were in this lower income group and this income included child support payments. Total expenditures on a child up to age 18 were, on average, 7 percent lower in single-parent households than in husband-wife households. But more single-parent than husband-wife families were in the bottom range of this income group. Average income for single-parent families in the lower income group was $26,350, compared with $38,000 for husband-wife families. Because single-parent families have one less potential earner, their total household income is lower and child-rearing expenses consume a greater percentage of income.

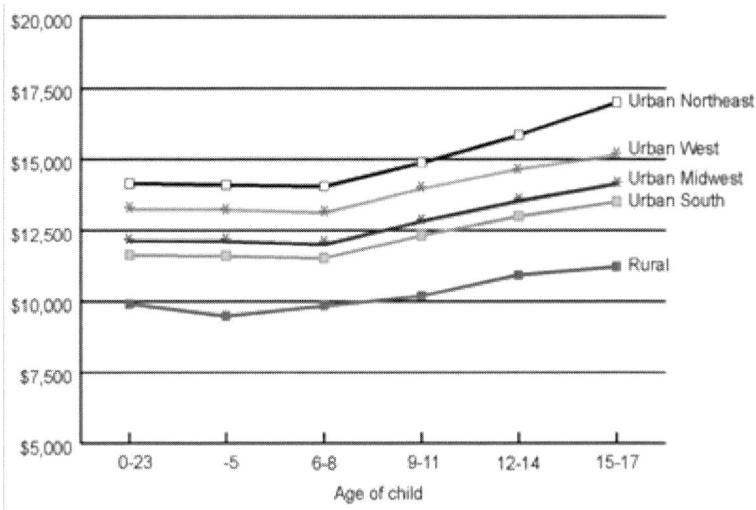

[1] Regional averages for the younger child in middle-income, husband-wife families with two children.

Figure 4. Family expenditures on a child, by region and age of child,1 2011.

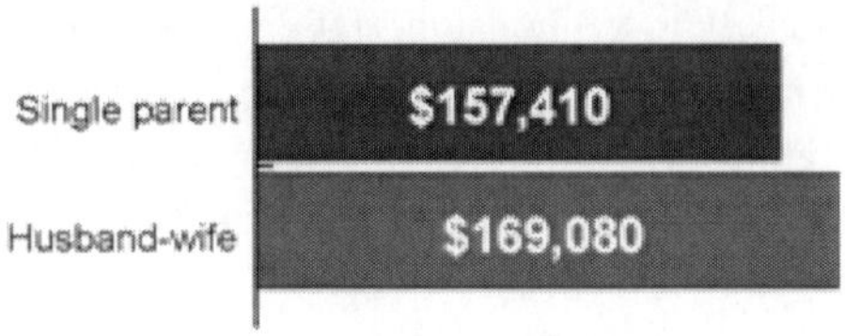

[1] U.S. average for the younger child in two-child families with before-tax income below $59,410.

Figure 5. Family expenditures on a child, by single-parent and husband-wife households, 1 2011.

For single parents, the estimates only cover out-of-pocket child-rearing expenditures made by the parent who has primary care of the child. The estimates do not include child-related expenditures made by the parent without primary care or by others, such as grandparents. The parent with whom the child does not reside the majority of the time may incur transportation, food, and entertainment expenses during visitation days and maintain a larger living unit because the child stays with him or her on weekends. The noncustodial parent could also contribute to the child's clothing and health care expenses. Although it would be ideal to include these expenditures, such expenditures could not be estimated from the CE data. Overall expenses paid by both parents on a child in a single-parent household, therefore, are likely to be greater than this study's estimates.

Adjustments for Older Children and Household Size

The estimates of expenses on children thus far represent expenditures on the younger children in a husband-wife and single-parent household with two children. Expenses on the older child may be different for the two family types. To determine the extent of this difference and how expenditures may be adjusted to estimate expenses on an older child, the USDA methodology to estimate expenditures on children was essentially repeated with the focus on an older child in each family type. Household income and region of residence (in the case of husband-wife households) were not controlled for, so findings apply to all families. The sample was smaller than that used for the principal analysis, since only households with all children age 17 or under were selected because the older child could not be over this age. The sample was weighted to reflect the U.S. population of interest.

It was found that tables 1-6 (pp. 26-31) reflect total expenditures on an older child in a husband- wife, two-child family, as well as on a younger child. Therefore, annual expenditures on children in a husband-wife, two-child family may be estimated by summing the total expenses for the specific age categories of the two children. For example, annual expenditures on a younger child age 11 and an older child age 16 in a husband-wife, two-child family in the middle- income group for the overall United States would be $27,430 (=$13,110 + $14,320) (table 8).

Table 8. Estimated annual expenditures on one, two, or three children by husband-wife and single-parent families, overall United States, 2011

Husband-wife family*		
One-child household		
Age of child		**Annual expenditure**
2		$12,370 x 1.25 = $15,460
5		12,390 x 1.25 = 15,490
8		12,290 x 1.25 = 15,360
11		13,110 x 1.25 = 16,390
14		13,820 x 1.25 = 17,280
17		14,320 x 1.25 = 17,900
Two-child household		
Age of younger child	**Age of older child**	
2	16	$12,370 + $14,320 = $26,690
5	16	12,390 + 14,320 = 26,710
8	16	12,290 + 14,320 = 26,610
11	16	13,110 + 14,320 = 27,430
14	16	13,820 + 14,320 = 28,140
15	16	14,320 + 14,320 = 28,640
Three-child household		
Age of youngest child	**Age of older children**	
2	13,16	($12,370 + $13,820 + $14,320) x .78 = $31,600
5	13,16	(12,390 + 13,820 + 14,320) x .78 = 31,610
8	13,16	(12,290 + 13,820 + 14,320) x .78 = 31,540
11	13,16	(13,110 + 13,820 + 14,320) x .78 = 32,180
12	13,16	(13,820 + 13,820 + 14,320) x .78 = 32,730

Table 8. (Continued)

Single-parent family**		
One-child household		
Age of child		**Annual expenditure**
2		$7,760 x 1.29 = $10,010
5		8,610 x 1.29 = 11,110
8		8,450 x 1.29 = 10,900
11		9,030 x 1.29 = 11,650
14		9,440 x 1.29 = 12,180
17		9,180 x 1.29 = 11,840
Two-child household		
Age of younger child	**Age of older child**	
2	16	$7,760 + ($9,180 x .97) = $16,660
5	16	8,610 + (9,180 x .97) = 17,510
8	16	8,450 + (9,180 x .97) = 17,350
11	16	9,030 + (9,180 x .97) = 17,930
14	16	9,440 + (9,180 x .97) = 18,340
15	16	9,180 + (9,180 x .97) = 18,080
Three-child household		
Age of youngest child	**Age of older children**	
2	13,16	($7,760 + ($9,440 x .97) + ($9,180 x .97)) x .77 = $19,880
5	13,16	(8,610 + (9,440 x .97) + (9,180 x .97)) x .77 = 20,540
8	13,16	(8,450 + (9,440 x .97) + (9,180 x .97)) x .77 = 20,410
11	13,16	(9,030 + (9,440 x .97) + (9,180 x .97)) x .77 = 20,860
12	13,16	(9,440 + (9,440 x .97) + (9,180 x .97)) x .77 = 21,180

* Estimates are for husband-wife families with 2011 before-tax income between $59,410 and $102,870.

** Estimates are for single-parent families with 2011 before-tax income less than $59,410.

Unlike husband-wife families, single-parent households with two children spend about 3 percent less on the older child than on the younger child at a specific age category. This reduced spending was largely due to less being spent on transportation and miscellaneous goods and services for the older child. Older children in single-parent families may be able to take less expensive public transportation rather than be driven by the parent in a car and forgo some items that the younger child has received. Also, some of these expenses may be covered by others not residing in the home. Therefore, annual expenditures on children in a single-parent, two-child family may be estimated from table 7 (p. 32) by: (1) taking the age category of the older child and adjusting the total expenses downward by 3 percent, and then (2) summing the total expenses for the specific age categories of the two children. For example, annual expenditures on a younger child age 8 and an older child age 16 in a single-parent, two-child family in the lower income group for the overall United States would be $17,350 (=$8,450 + ($9,180 X.97)) (table 8). It should be noted that for specific budgetary components, annual expenses on an older child in husband-wife and single-parent families varied, compared with those on a younger child in a two-child family.

The estimates should also be adjusted if a household has only one child or more than two children. Families will spend more or less on a child, depending on the number of other children in the household (income being spread over fewer or more children) and as a result of economies of scale. To derive these adjustments, the USDA methodology to estimate expenditures on children was replicated for both husband-wife and single-parent families with one child and three or more children. The maximum number of children was restricted to three or more because only a small percentage of families had four or more children.

Household income and region of residence (in the case of husband-wife households) were not controlled for, so findings apply to all families. For families with three or more children, the possibility of children sharing a bedroom was factored in by examining the number of bedrooms and number of children in the household.

Compared with expenditures for each child in a husband-wife, two-child family, husband-wife households with one child spend an average of 25 percent more on the single child, and those with three or more children spend an average of 22 percent less on each child. For single- parent families, those with one child spend an average of 29 percent more on the single child than on a child in a two-child family, and those with three or more children spend an average of 23 percent less on each child. As families have more children, the children can share a bedroom, clothing and toys can be handed down to younger children, food can be purchased in larger and more economical packages, and private schools or child care centers may offer sibling discounts.

Therefore, to estimate annual overall expenditures on an only child by using data in tables 1-7, 25 percent should be added to the total expense for each age category for husband-wife families and 29 percent should be added to the total expense for each age category for single-parent families. To estimate expenses on three or more children in husband-wife families, 22 percent should be subtracted from the total expense for each child's age category and these totals should be summed. For single-parent families with three or more children, 23 percent should be subtracted from the total expense for each child's age category (after adjusting the expenses on the older children downward), and these totals should be summed. These percentages may be more or less for a particular budgetary component for both family types. As family size increases, costs per child for food decrease less than for housing and transportation. Much housing space is used in common, and car trips can serve more than one child.

As an example of adjustments needed for different numbers of children, consider total expenses on children in husband-wife families with one, two, and three children (presented in table 8 for a household with before-tax income between $59,410 and $102,870). In the example, the age of the older child is 16 in the two-child household and the ages of the older children are 13 and 16 in the three-child household. As can be seen, less is spent per child as family size increases. The estimated annual expense on a child age 2 with no siblings is $15,460; for two children ages 2 and 16, $26,690; and for three children ages 2, 13, and 16, $31,600. Table 8 also shows the expenditure adjustments needed for children in single-parent families with one, two, and three children and with a before-tax income below $59,410. The major difference in the mechanics of the adjustment for single-parent, compared with husband-wife households, is that the expenses on older children need to be adjusted downward by 3 percent.

Alternative Estimates of Expenditures on Children

The USDA methodology to estimate child-rearing expenses is based on several steps: (1) assigning child-specific expenses (clothing, child care, and education) in the CE data to children, (2) allocating household-level expenses based on findings from authoritative research (food and health care) or on a per capita basis (transportation and miscellaneous items), and (3) calculating housing expenses by using an approach that accounts for the average cost of an additional bedroom. An alternative method to estimate expenditures on children is a marginal cost method. The marginal cost method measures expenditures on children as the difference in expenses between families with children and equivalent families without children. While there is no generally accepted equivalency measure in the economics literature, two of the most commonly used are the Engel and Rothbarth approaches. The Engel approach assumes that if two families spend an equal percentage of their total expenditures on food, they are equally well-off. The Rothbarth approach assumes that if two families spend an equal amount on luxuries (e.g., alcohol, tobacco, entertainment, and sweets) and have the same level of savings, they are equally well-off. (See U.S. Department of Health and Human Services, 1990, for more detailed information on these two approaches.)

One limitation of the Engel and Rothbarth estimators is that they are not true marginal cost approaches. A true marginal cost approach examines additional expenditures a family makes because of the presence of a child in the household—how much more the family spends on housing, food, and other items because of the child. A true marginal cost approach would track the same sample of families over time. Marginal cost approaches, as implemented, do not do this. They examine two different sets of families, those with children and those without children, at one point in time. Hence, the term "marginal cost approach" is somewhat of a misnomer.

Another limitation with the marginal cost approach is that it does not consider substitution effects. It assumes parents do not alter their expenditures on themselves after a child is added to a household. This could lead to problems when applying the marginal cost method to individual budgetary components. For example, many families may reduce the number of high-cost vacations they take once they have children. However, with the marginal cost method, transportation expenses of these families without children would be compared with expenses of families with children, likely leading to underestimates of transportation expenses on a child.

These problems with the marginal cost method are likely more severe if used to calculate miscellaneous expenses on a child. Published data show entertainment expenses, one of the major components of the miscellaneous category, were greater for husband-wife couples without children than for husband-wife families with young children (U.S. Department of Labor, 2008). Using the marginal cost method in this case could lead to the questionable result of having negative entertainment expenditures on a child. The household entertainment expenses of husband-wife couples without children were about the same as those of husband- wife families with an oldest child over age 18 living in the household, suggesting a miniscule expenditure on a child (U.S. Department of Labor, 2008).

Table 9. Average percent of household expenditures attributable to children in husband-wife families, by estimator and number of children

Number of children	One	Two	Three
	Percent		
Estimator			
Engel (2001)[1]	30	44	52
Rothbarth (2001)[1]	26	36	42
Rothbarth (2006)[2]	25	37	44
Engel (2008)[3]	21	31	38
Rothbarth (2008)[3]	32	47	57
Rothbarth (2011)[4]	24	37	45
Average of above	26	39	46
USDA (2012)	27	41	47

[1] From Judicial Council of California (2001).
[2] From Policy Studies Inc. (2006).
[3] From McCaleb, Macpherson, and Norrbin (2008).
[4] From Judicial Council of California (2011).

Since 2000, several studies have estimated child-rearing expenses by using both the Engel and Rothbarth estimators and applying them to Consumer Expenditure Survey data. Table 9 shows the child-rearing expense estimates produced by these studies for husband-wife families by number of children and as a percentage of total family expenditures; these studies estimated child-rearing expenses as a percentage of total expenditures and did not examine expenses by budgetary component. It should be noted that the Rothbarth method was usually implemented by using only adult clothing as the equivalency method so is not a full implementation of the Rothbarth approach. Hence, how results would differ if a more complete Rothbarth approach were implemented is unknown. An earlier study found the results of the Rothbarth approach to vary considerably depending on the budgetary items included in the equivalency scale definition and concluded this revealed a significant weakness in the practical application of the approach (Lancaster and Ray, 1998).

What is striking is the range in estimates resulting from the various studies. For one child, the estimates ranged between 21 to 32 percent of household expenditures being spent on the child; for two children, 31 to 47 percent; and for three children, 38 to 57 percent (almost a 20-percentage- point difference). When using the marginal cost method in estimating expenditures on children, a researcher's choice of an equivalency scale is crucial because different measures yield different results. Even using the same equivalency measure can result in different estimates, depending on the years of data used and model specification. For example, the 2011 study based on the Rothbarth estimator found that for two-child families, 37 percent of total family expenditures went to goods and services for children (Judicial Council of California, 2011), while the 2008 study using the Rothbarth estimator found that 47 percent of expenditures went to goods and services for two children (McCaleb et al., 2008). The 2008 study found the Rothbarth estimator to be the most sensitive to underlying data and sample restrictions. Also, the 2011 study calls into question the validity of the Engel approach.

So, how do the USDA child-rearing expense estimates compare with the results of these studies? Table 9 presents the USDA (2012) estimates. Because the studies implementing the Engel and Rothbarth techniques usually did not include personal insurance and pension contributions in total household expenditures, when calculating the USDA child-rearing expenses as a percentage of total household expenditures, these two budgetary components were not included. Also, the marginal cost methods include families with child care/education expenses and families without child care/education expenses and many do not include mortgage principal payments, so the USDA estimates in table 9 are based on average child care/education expenses for all husband-wife families, including those without the expense, and do not include mortgage principal, which constitutes about 15 percent of overall housing expenses. This differs from the USDA child-rearing expenditure estimates in tables 1-7, where mortgage principal payments are included in housing expenses and where child care/education expenses are only for families incurring the expense. If mortgage principal was included, the USDA estimates on table 9 would be 2 percentage points higher for one-child and two-children families (29 and 43 percent) and 3 percentage points higher for three-children families (50 percent).

For husband-wife families with one child, USDA estimates 27 percent of total family expendi tures are spent on the child; for two children, 41 percent; and for three children, 47 percent. These percentages are very near the averages of the various studies using the Engel and Rothbarth approaches. One factor the various approaches have in common is that expenditures on children do not increase proportionately as the number of children increases; expenditures on two children are less than twice as much as those on one child.

Table 10. Estimated annual expenditures* on a child born in 2011, by income group, overall United States

Year	Age	Income group		
		Lowest	Middle	Highest
2011	<1	$9,050	$12,370	$20,460
2012	1	9,280	12,690	20,980
2013	2	9,520	13,010	21,520
2014	3	9,810	13,360	22,090
2015	4	10,060	13,700	22,650
2016	5	10,320	14,050	23,230
2017	6	10,190	14,290	23,750
2018	7	10,450	14,660	24,360
2019	8	10,710	15,030	24,980
2020	9	11,940	16,440	26,740
2021	10	12,250	16,860	27,420
2022	11	12,560	17,290	28,120
2023	12	13,470	18,700	30,710
2024	13	13,820	19,170	31,490
2025	14	14,170	19,660	32,290
2026	15	14,550	20,890	35,760
2027	16	14,920	21,420	36,670
2028	17	15,300	21,970	37,610
Total		**$212,370**	**$295,560**	**$490,830**

* Estimates are for the younger child in husband-wife families with two children and assume an average annual inflation rate of 2.55 percent.

Estimating Future Costs

The estimates presented so far represent household expenditures on a child of a certain age in 2011. What would be the total expenses on a child born in 2011 through age 17, factoring in inflation? To estimate these expenses over time, future price changes need to be incorporated. To do this, a future cost formula is used:

$$C_f = C_p (1 + i)^n$$

Where:

C_f = projected future annual dollar expenditure on a child of a particular age

C_p = present (2011) annual dollar expenditure on a child of a particular age
i = projected annual inflation (or deflation) rate
n = number of years from present until child will reach a particular age

An example of estimated future expenditures on the younger child in a husband-wife family with two children is presented in table 10. The example assumes a child is born in 2011 and reaches age 17 in the year 2028, and the average annual inflation rate over this time is 2.55 percent (the average annual inflation rate over the past 20 years) (U.S. Department of Labor, 2012). As can be seen, total family expenses on a child through age 17 would be $212,370 for households in the lowest income group, $295,560 for those in the middle, and $490,830 for those in the highest income group. In 2011 dollar values, these figures would be $169,080, $234,900, and $389,670, respectively.

Inflation rates other than 2.55 percent could be used in the formula if inflation projections change. Also, it is somewhat unrealistic to assume that households remain in one income category as a child grows older. For most families, income rises over time, so a family may move from one income group to another. In addition, such inflation projections assume child- rearing expenditures change only with inflation. Parental expenditure patterns also change over time.

Expenditures Not Included

Expenditures estimated in this study consisted of direct parental expenses made on children through age 17 for seven major budgetary components. These expenditures exclude costs related to prenatal health care. The expenditures also exclude costs made on children after age 17. One of the largest of these excluded expenses is the cost of a college education. The College Board (2012) estimated that in 2011-2012, annual average (enrollment-weighted) tuition and fees were $8,244 at 4-year public colleges (in-State tuition) and $28,500 at 4-year private (non-profit) colleges; annual room and board was $8,887 at 4-year public colleges and $10,089 at 4-year private colleges. For 2-year colleges in 2011-2012, annual average tuition and fees were $2,963 at public colleges. These college costs may be offset by financial aid. College-related expenses on children may even take place before children are college age in the form of savings. Other parental expenses on children after age 17 could include those associated with children living at home or if children do not live at home, gifts and other contributions to them. Expenses related to life insurance on parents are not included in the estimates. Although these expenses are not made directly on children, it is likely that they are primarily incurred for the benefit of children.

EXPENDITURES ON CHILDREN: 1960 VERSUS 2011

The U.S. Department of Agriculture first provided estimates of child-rearing expenditures in 1960. The current estimates are not precisely comparable to previous estimates because of methodology changes; for example, housing expenses are now determined by using the average cost of an additional bedroom as opposed to a per capita approach, and food expenses are now based on what households spend as opposed to a suggested standard. Although these types of methodological changes exist, a general comparison is possible.

In 1960, average expenditures on a child in a middle-income, husband-wife family amounted to $25,229, or $191,723 in 2011 dollars (figure). By 2011, these estimated expenditures climbed 23 percent in real terms to $234,900 (assuming a family had child care and education expenses on a child). Housing was the largest expense on a child in both time periods and increased in real terms over this time. Food was also one of the largest expenses in both time periods, but decreased in real terms. Changes in agriculture over the past 50 years have resulted in family food budgets being a lower percentage of household income. Transportation expenses on a child increased slightly in real terms from 1960 to 2011.

Clothing and miscellaneous expenses on a child decreased as a percentage of total child-rearing expenses and in real terms from 1960 to 2011. Reduced real expenses on children's clothing is somewhat of a surprise given the popularity of many designer clothing items today; however, it is likely that technological changes and globalization have made clothing less expensive in real terms. The growth in real terms of housing and other expenses on a child may be the cause of the decline in miscellaneous expenses on a child, which are often seen as discretionary.

Health care expenses on a child doubled as a percentage of total child-rearing costs, as well as increasing in real terms, from 1960 to 2011. The dramatic rise in health care costs over time has received widespread attention. Perhaps the most striking change in child- rearing expenses over time relates to child care and education expenses.

It should be noted that in 1960, child care/education expenses included families with and without the expense. Even so, these expenses grew from 2 percent of total child-rearing expenditures in 1960 (for families with and without the expense) to 18 percent (for families with the expense) in 2011. Much of this growth is likely related to child care. In 1960, child care costs were negligible, mainly consisting of in-the-home babysitting. Since then, the labor force participation of women has greatly increased, leading to the need for more child care. Child-rearing expense estimates were not provided for single-parent families in 1960, likely because of the small percentage of children residing in such households at the time.

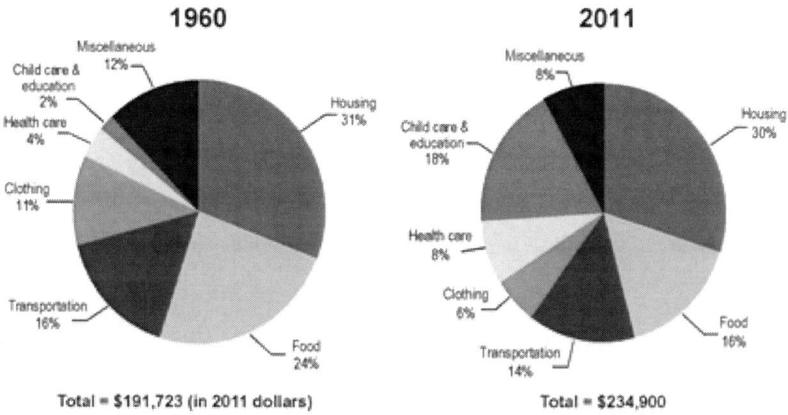

[1] U.S. average for a child in middle-income, husband-wife families.

Figure. Expenditures on a child from birth through age 17, total expenses and budgetary component shares, 1960 versus 2011.[1]

The estimates do not include all government expenditures on children. Examples of excluded expenses would be public education, Medicaid, and subsidized school meals. The actual expenditures on children (by parents and the government), therefore, would be higher than reported in this study, especially for children in the lowest income group. Expenditures on children made by people not in the household, such as grandparents and other relatives, were also not factored in the estimates. Indirect costs involved in child rearing were not included in the estimates. Although these costs are typically more difficult to measure than direct expenditures, they may be substantial. The time involved in rearing children is considerable and has a cost attached to it.

A recent study found that the imputed value of parental time spent on children exceeded the direct cash expenditures on them (Folbre, 2008). In addition, to care for children, current earnings and future career opportunities may be diminished because of job choice or reduced time in the labor force for one or both parents. These situations also have a cost attached to them.

The direct and indirect costs of raising children are considerable, absorbing a major share of the household budget. On the other hand, these costs may be outweighed by the benefits of children.

REFERENCES

Bernard, D. (2007). *Out-of-Pocket Expenditures on Health Care Among the Nonelderly Population, 2004.* (Statistical Brief #159). Agency for Healthcare Research and Quality, Rockville, MD: Department of Health and Human Services.

Dublin, L. I. & Lotka, A. J. (1946). *The Money Value of a Man.* New York City, NY: Ronald Press. Folbre, N. (2008). *Valuing Children: Rethinking the Economics of the Family.* Cambridge, MA: Harvard University Press.

The College Board. (2012). *Trends in College Pricing 2011.* Retrieved March 23, 2012, from http://trends.collegeboard.org/college_pricing/report_findings/indicator/910#f8002.

Hu, P. S & Reuscher, T. R. (2004). *Summary of Travel Trends: 2001 National Household Travel Survey.* Washington, DC: U.S. Department of Transportation, Federal Highway Administration.

Judicial Council of California. (2001). *Review of Statewide Uniform Child Support Guideline.* Retrieved March 27, 2009 at http://www.courtinfo.ca.gov/programs/cfcc/pdffiles/ChildSupport-2001UniformChildSupport Guideline.pdf.

Judicial Council of California. (2011). *Review of Statewide Uniform Child Support Guideline 2010.* Retrieved March 14, 2012, from http://www.courts.ca.gov/documents/review-sucsg-0611.pdf.

Lancaster, G. & Ray, R. (1998). Comparison of alternative models of household equivalence scales: The Australian evidence on unit record data. *The Economic Record, 74*(224), 1-14.

Lino, M. & Carlson, A. (2010). Estimating housing expenses on children: A comparison of methodologies. *Journal of Legal Economics, 16*(2), 61-79.

Lino, M. (2008). *Expenditures on Children by Families, 2007.* U.S. Department of Agriculture, Center for Nutrition Policy and Promotion. (Miscellaneous Publication Number 1528-2007).

McCaleb, T. S., Macpherson, D. A. & Norrbin, S. C. (2008). *Review and Update of Florida's Child Support Guidelines.* Report to the Florida Legislature, November17, 2008.

McDonald, J .F. & Moffitt, R. A. (1980). The uses of Tobit analysis. *The Review of Economics and Statistics, 62*(2), 318-321.

PiperJaffray. (2010). *Piper Jaffray Completes 19th Semiannual Spring 2010 Taking Stock With Teens Survey.* Retrieved March 4, 2011, from http://www.piperjaffray.com/1col.aspx?id=287&releaseid=1412443&title =Piper%20Jaffray.

Policy Studies Inc. (Venohr, J., Betson, D., Price, D., Zoller, M., & Washington, L.) (2006). *State of Oregon Child Support Guidelines Review: Updated Obligation Scales and Other Considerations.* Submitted to Department of Justice, Division of Child Support on June 26, 2006.

U.S. Census Bureau. (2011). Who's Minding the Kids? Child Care Arrangements: Spring 2010—Detailed Tables. Retrieved March 7, 2012, from http://www.census.gov/hhes/childcare/ data/sipp/2010/tables.html.

U.S. Department of Agriculture, Agricultural Research Service. (1981). *USDA Estimates of the Cost of Raising a Child: A Guide to Their Use and Interpretation.* (Miscellaneous Publication No. 1411).

U.S. Department of Agriculture, Center for Nutrition Policy and Promotion. (2008). *Official USDA Food Plans: Cost of Food at Home at Four Levels, U.S. Average, March 2008.* Alexandria, VA.

U.S. Department of Health and Human Services, Office of the Assistant Secretary for Planning and Evaluation. (1990). *Estimates of Expenditures on Children and Child Support Guidelines.*

U.S. Department of Labor, Bureau of Labor Statistics. (2007). *2005 Consumer Expenditure Interview Survey Public Use Microdata Documentation.*

U.S. Department of Labor, Bureau of Labor Statistics. (2008). *Composition of Consumer Unit: Average Annual Expenditures and Characteristics, Consumer Expenditure Survey, 2006.* Retrieved November 5, 2008, from http://www.bls.gov/cex/2006/Standard/cucomp.pdf.

U.S. Department of Labor, Bureau of Labor Statistics. (2012). *Consumer Price Index.* Retrieved March 16, 2012, from ftp://ftp.bls.gov/pub/special. requests/cpi/cpiai.txt.

INDEX

A

B

C

D

E

F

G

H

I

L

M

O

P

R

S

T

U

V

W

Y